DECLASSIFIED

Report of Proceedings
volume 3

QUEEN & COUNTRY™

DECLASSIFIED

Report of Proceedings
volume 3

written by **ANTONY JOHNSTON**

illustrated by **CHRISTOPHER MITTEN**

series creator & consultant **GREG RUCKA**

covers and chapter breaks by
CHRISTOPHER MITTEN

lettering by
JOHN DRANSKI

book design by
KEITH WOOD

edited by
RANDAL C. JARRELL

Published by Oni Press, Inc.
JOE NOZEMACK, publisher
JAMES LUCAS JONES, editor in chief
RANDAL C. JARRELL, managing editor
MARYANNE SNELL, director of marketing & sales
DOUGLAS SHERWOOD, editorial intern

Original Queen & Country logo designed by
STEVEN BIRCH @ Servo

This collects issues 1-3 of the Oni Press comics series
Queen & Country™: Declassified volume 3.

ONI PRESS, INC.
1305 SE Martin Luther King JR. Blvd.
Suite A
Portland, OR 97214
USA

www.onipress.com • www.gregrucka.com
www.mostlyblack.com • www.christophermitten.com

First edition: March 2006
ISBN 1-932664-35-1

1 3 5 7 9 10 8 6 4 2

PRINTED IN CANADA.

CHAPTER 1

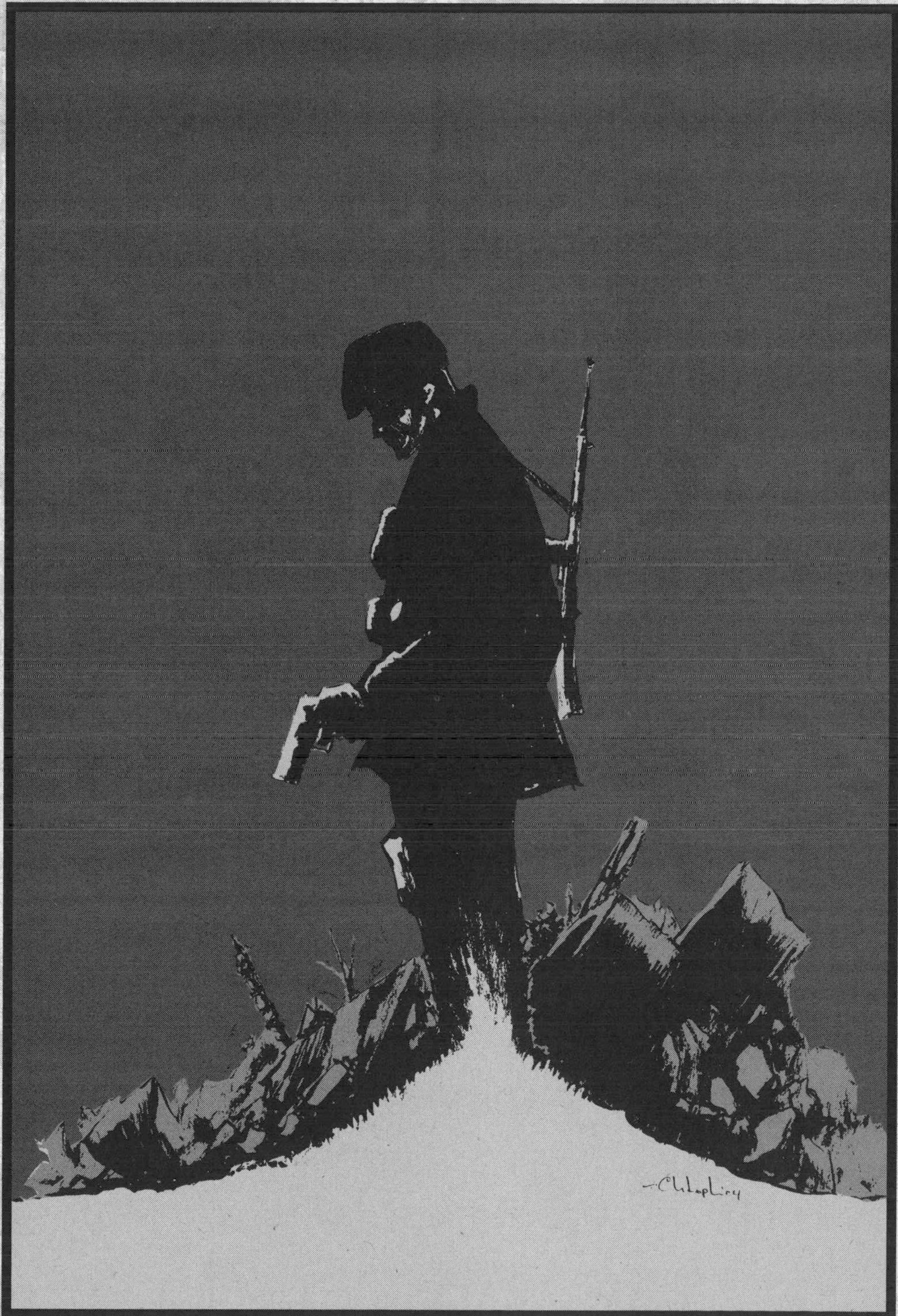

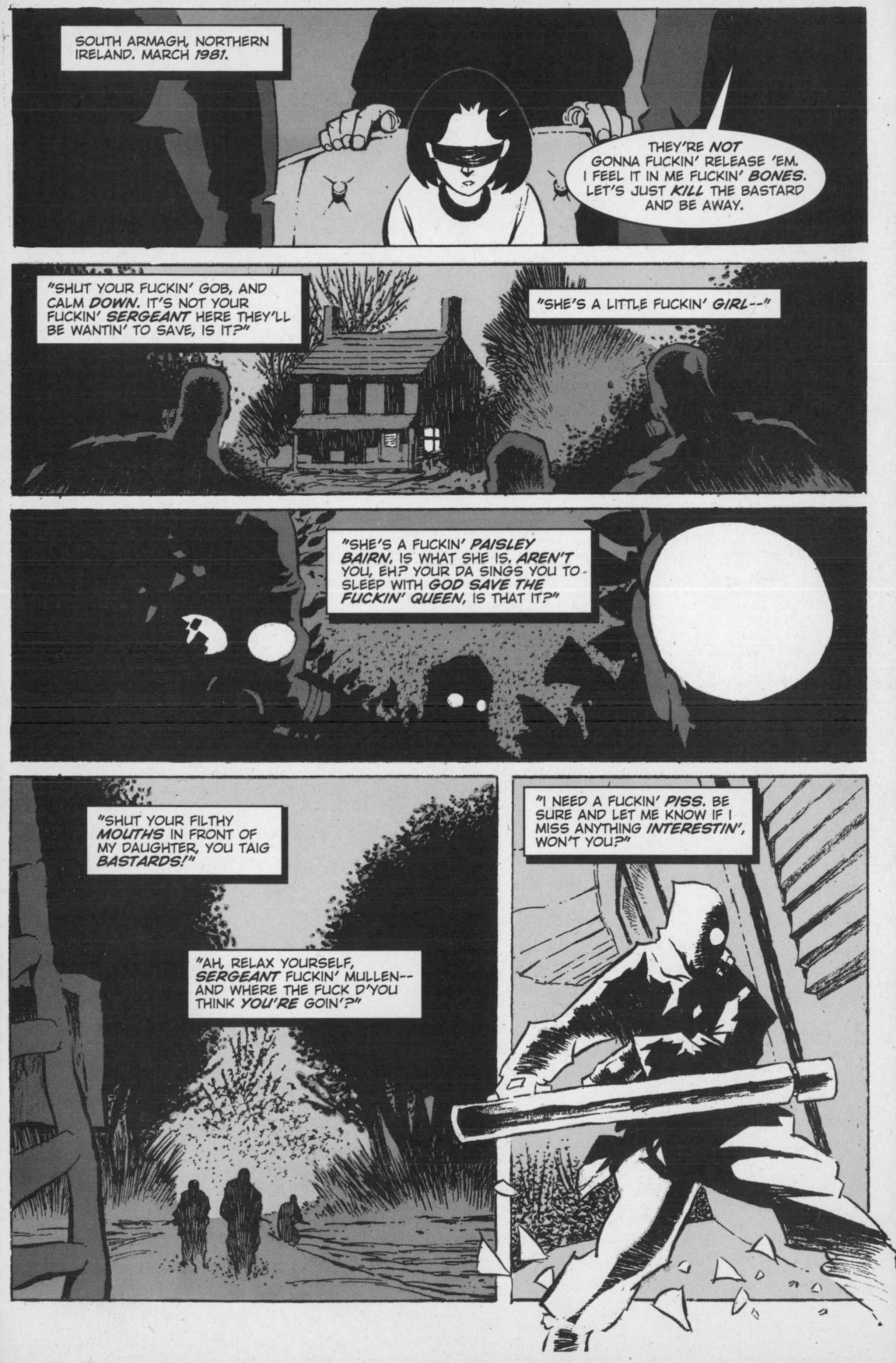
SOUTH ARMAGH, NORTHERN IRELAND. MARCH 1981.
THEY'RE NOT GONNA FUCKIN' RELEASE 'EM. I FEEL IT IN ME FUCKIN' BONES. LET'S JUST KILL THE BASTARD AND BE AWAY.
"SHUT YOUR FUCKIN' GOB, AND CALM DOWN. IT'S NOT YOUR FUCKIN' SERGEANT HERE THEY'LL BE WANTIN' TO SAVE, IS IT?"
"SHE'S A LITTLE FUCKIN' GIRL--"
"SHE'S A FUCKIN' PAISLEY BAIRN, IS WHAT SHE IS. AREN'T YOU, EH? YOUR DA SINGS YOU TO SLEEP WITH GOD SAVE THE FUCKIN' QUEEN, IS THAT IT?"
"SHUT YOUR FILTHY MOUTHS IN FRONT OF MY DAUGHTER, YOU TAIG BASTARDS!"
"AH, RELAX YOURSELF, SERGEANT FUCKIN' MULLEN-- AND WHERE THE FUCK D'YOU THINK YOU'RE GOIN'?"
"I NEED A FUCKIN' PISS. BE SURE AND LET ME KNOW IF I MISS ANYTHING INTERESTIN', WON'T YOU?"

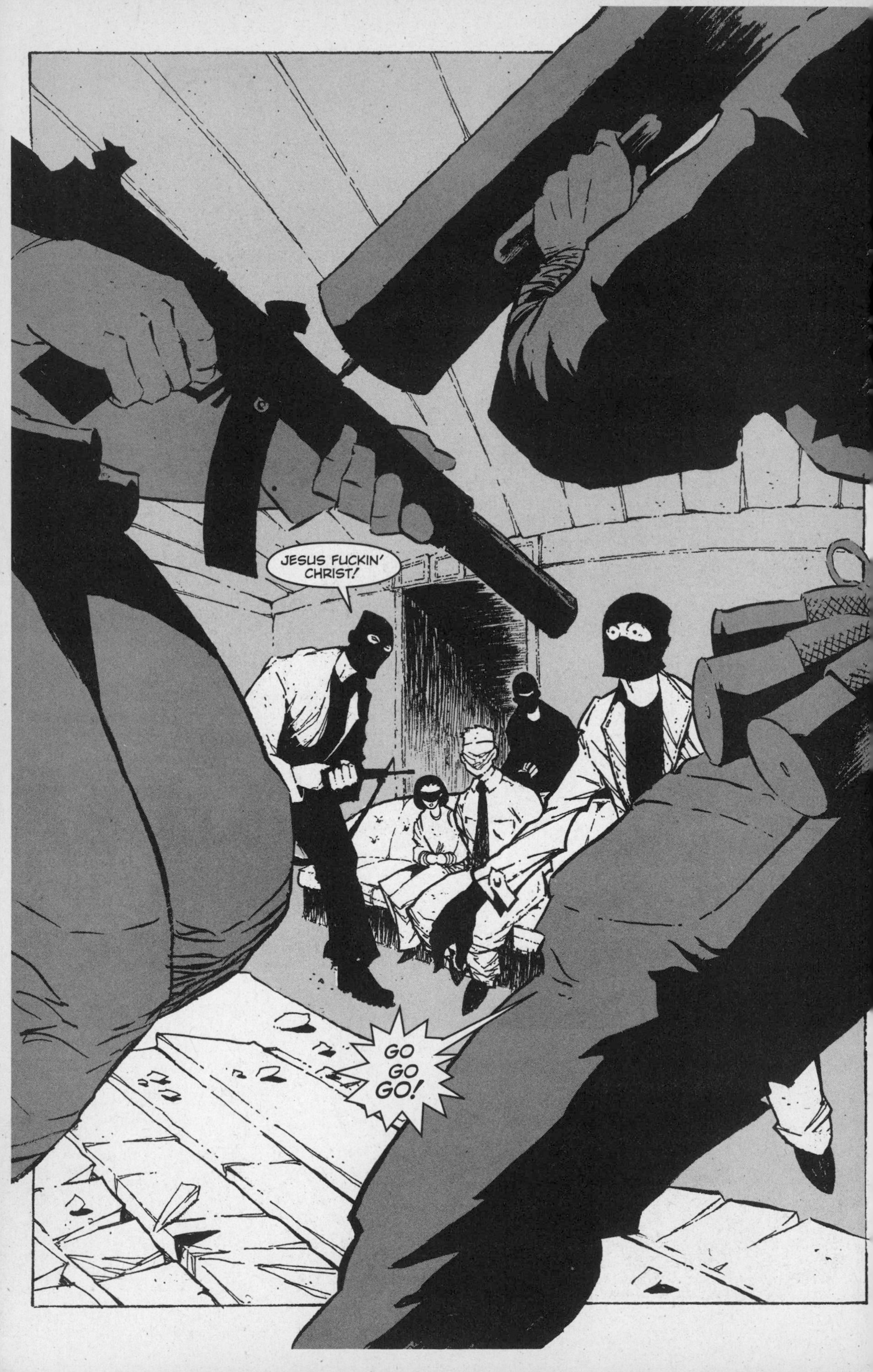
JESUS FUCKIN' CHRIST!
GO GO GO!

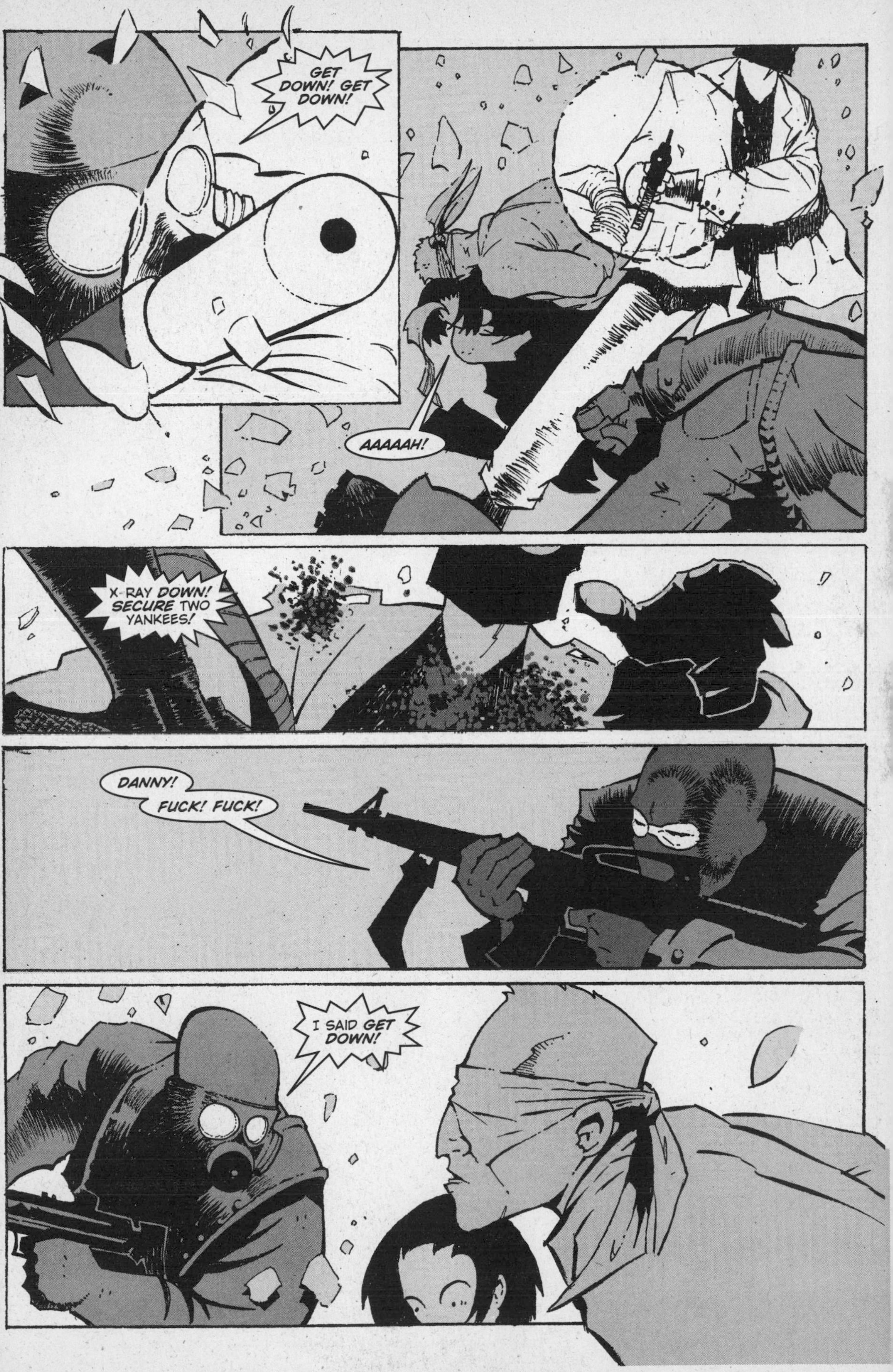
GET DOWN! GET DOWN!
AAAAAH!
X-RAY DOWN! SECURE TWO YANKEES!
DANNY!
FUCK! FUCK!
I SAID GET DOWN!

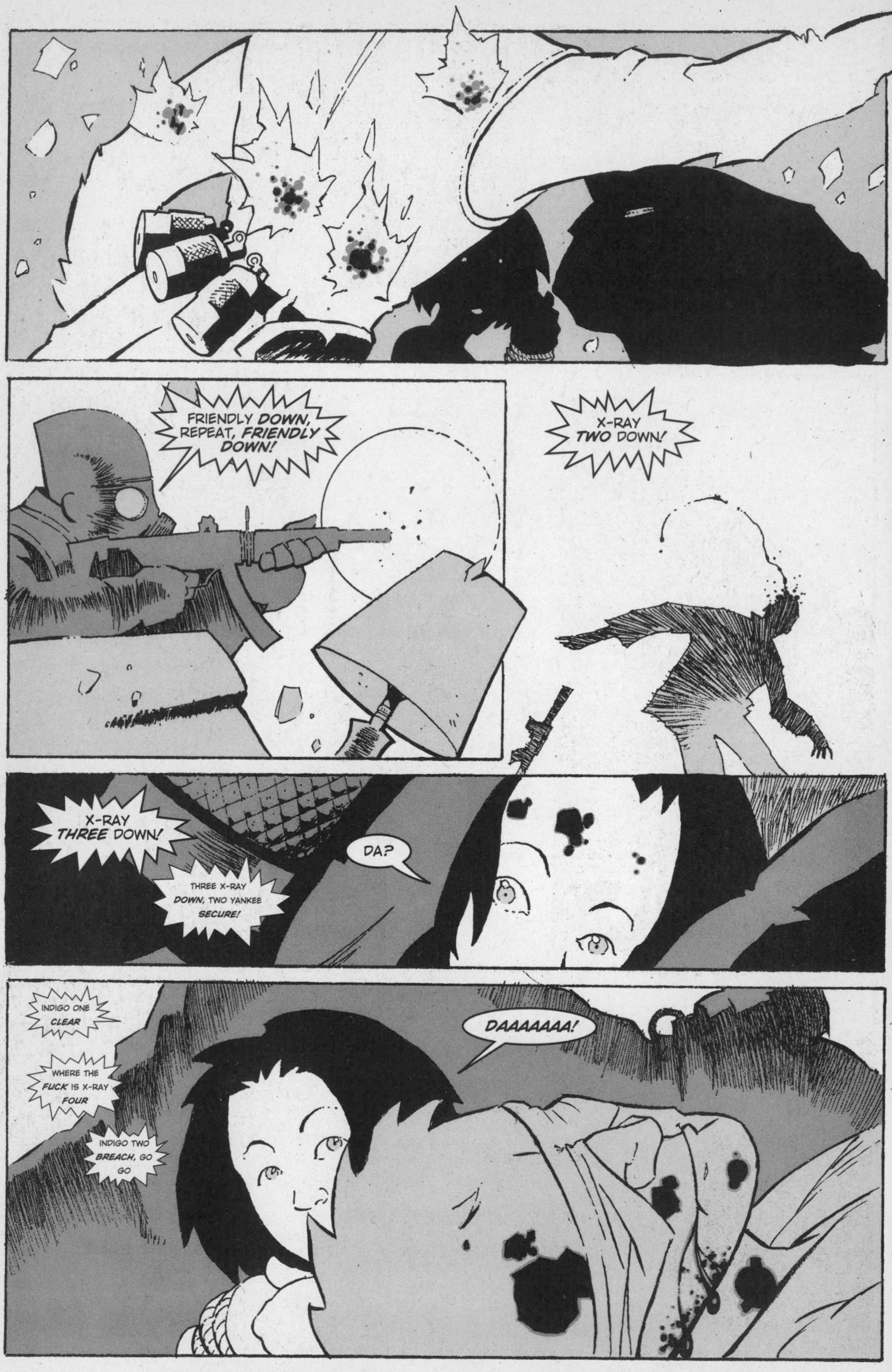
FRIENDLY DOWN, REPEAT, FRIENDLY DOWN!
X-RAY TWO DOWN!
X-RAY THREE DOWN!
DA?
THREE X-RAY DOWN, TWO YANKEE SECURE!
INDIGO ONE CLEAR
DAAAAAAA!
WHERE THE FUCK IS X-RAY FOUR
INDIGO TWO BREACH, GO GO

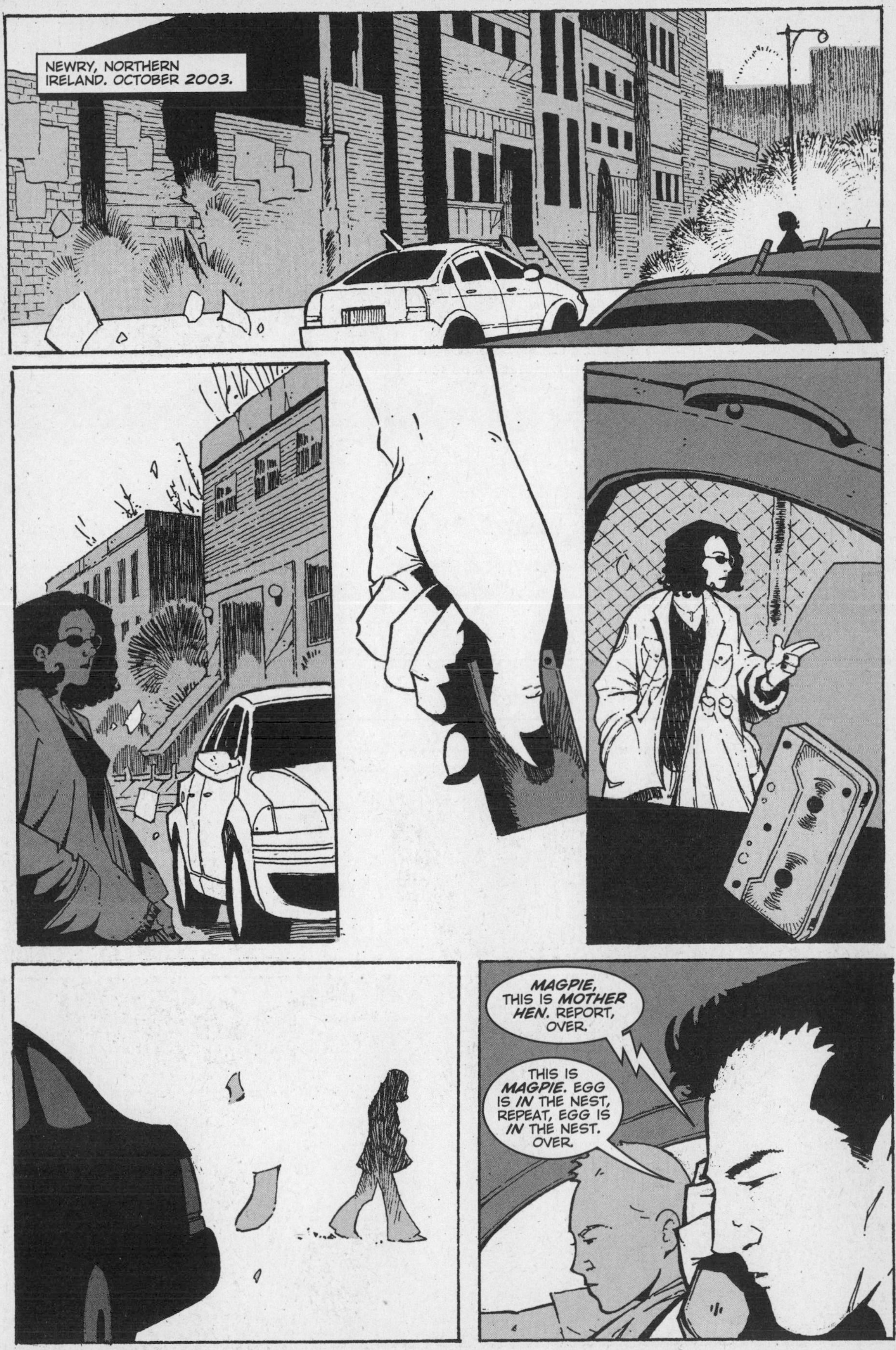
NEWRY, NORTHERN IRELAND. OCTOBER 2003.
MAGPIE, THIS IS MOTHER HEN. REPORT, OVER.
THIS IS MAGPIE. EGG IS IN THE NEST, REPEAT, EGG IS IN THE NEST. OVER.

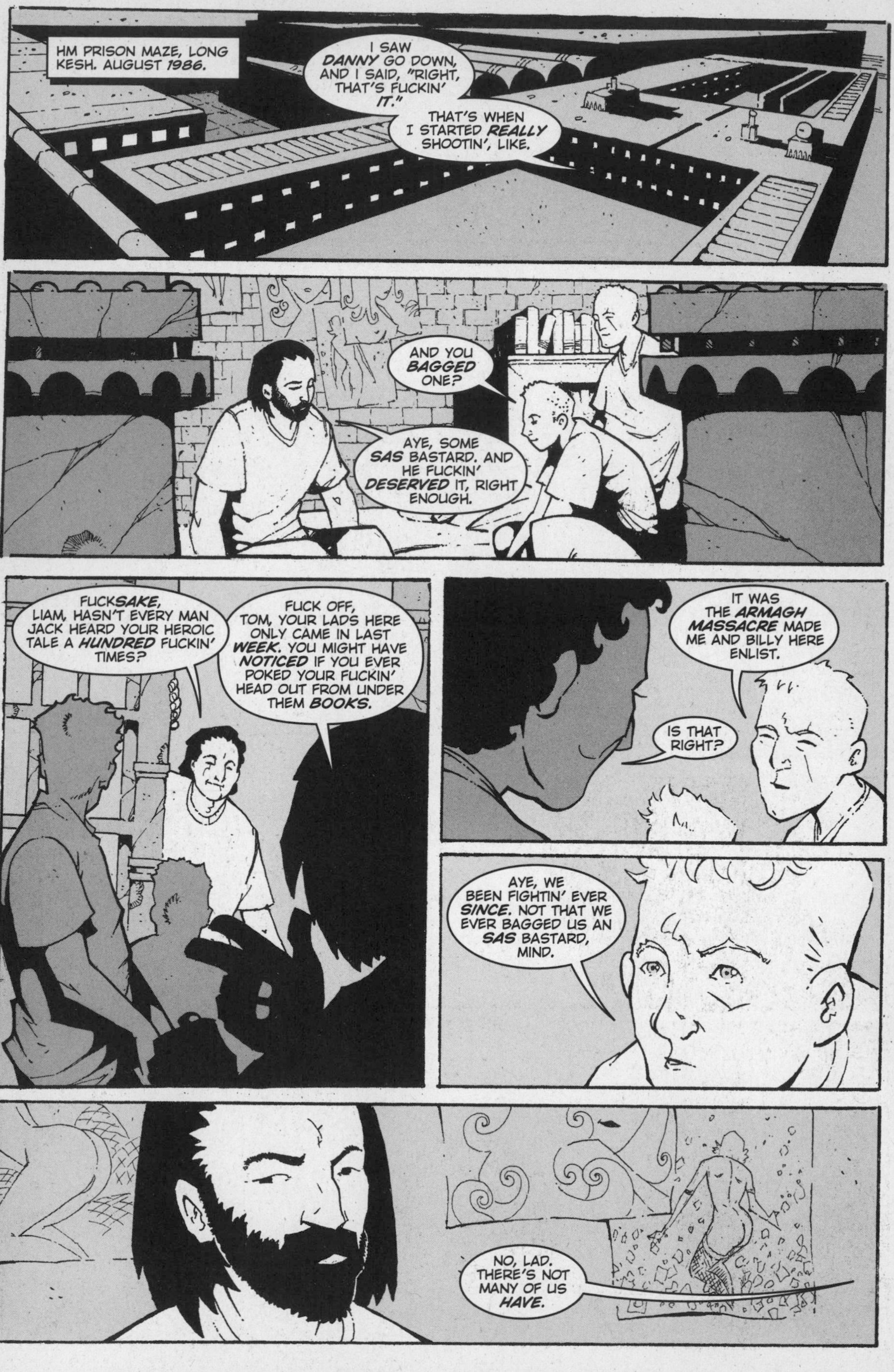
HM PRISON MAZE, LONG KESH. AUGUST 1986.
I SAW DANNY GO DOWN, AND I SAID, "RIGHT, THAT'S FUCKIN' IT."
THAT'S WHEN I STARTED REALLY SHOOTIN', LIKE.
AND YOU BAGGED ONE?
AYE, SOME SAS BASTARD. AND HE FUCKIN' DESERVED IT, RIGHT ENOUGH.
FUCKSAKE, LIAM, HASN'T EVERY MAN JACK HEARD YOUR HEROIC TALE A HUNDRED FUCKIN' TIMES?
FUCK OFF, TOM, YOUR LADS HERE ONLY CAME IN LAST WEEK. YOU MIGHT HAVE NOTICED IF YOU EVER POKED YOUR FUCKIN' HEAD OUT FROM UNDER THEM BOOKS.
IT WAS THE ARMAGH MASSACRE MADE ME AND BILLY HERE ENLIST.
IS THAT RIGHT?
AYE, WE BEEN FIGHTIN' EVER SINCE. NOT THAT WE EVER BAGGED US AN SAS BASTARD, MIND.
NO, LAD. THERE'S NOT MANY OF US HAVE.

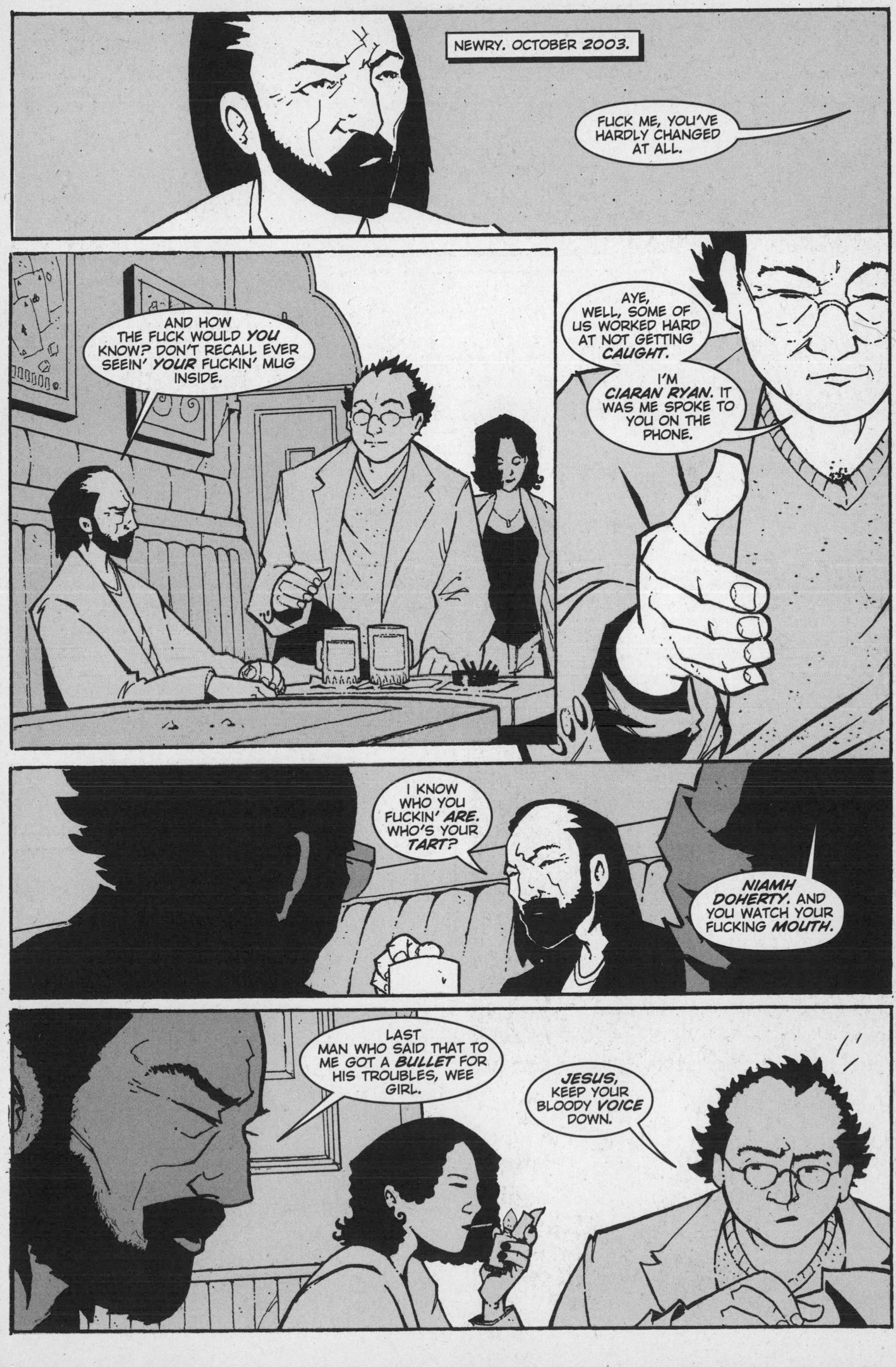
NEWRY. OCTOBER 2003.
FUCK ME, YOU'VE HARDLY CHANGED AT ALL.
AND HOW THE FUCK WOULD YOU KNOW? DON'T RECALL EVER SEEIN' YOUR FUCKIN' MUG INSIDE.
AYE, WELL, SOME OF US WORKED HARD AT NOT GETTING CAUGHT.
I'M CIARAN RYAN. IT WAS ME SPOKE TO YOU ON THE PHONE.
I KNOW WHO YOU FUCKIN' ARE. WHO'S YOUR TART?
NIAMH DOHERTY. AND YOU WATCH YOUR FUCKING MOUTH.
LAST MAN WHO SAID THAT TO ME GOT A BULLET FOR HIS TROUBLES, WEE GIRL.
JESUS, KEEP YOUR BLOODY VOICE DOWN.

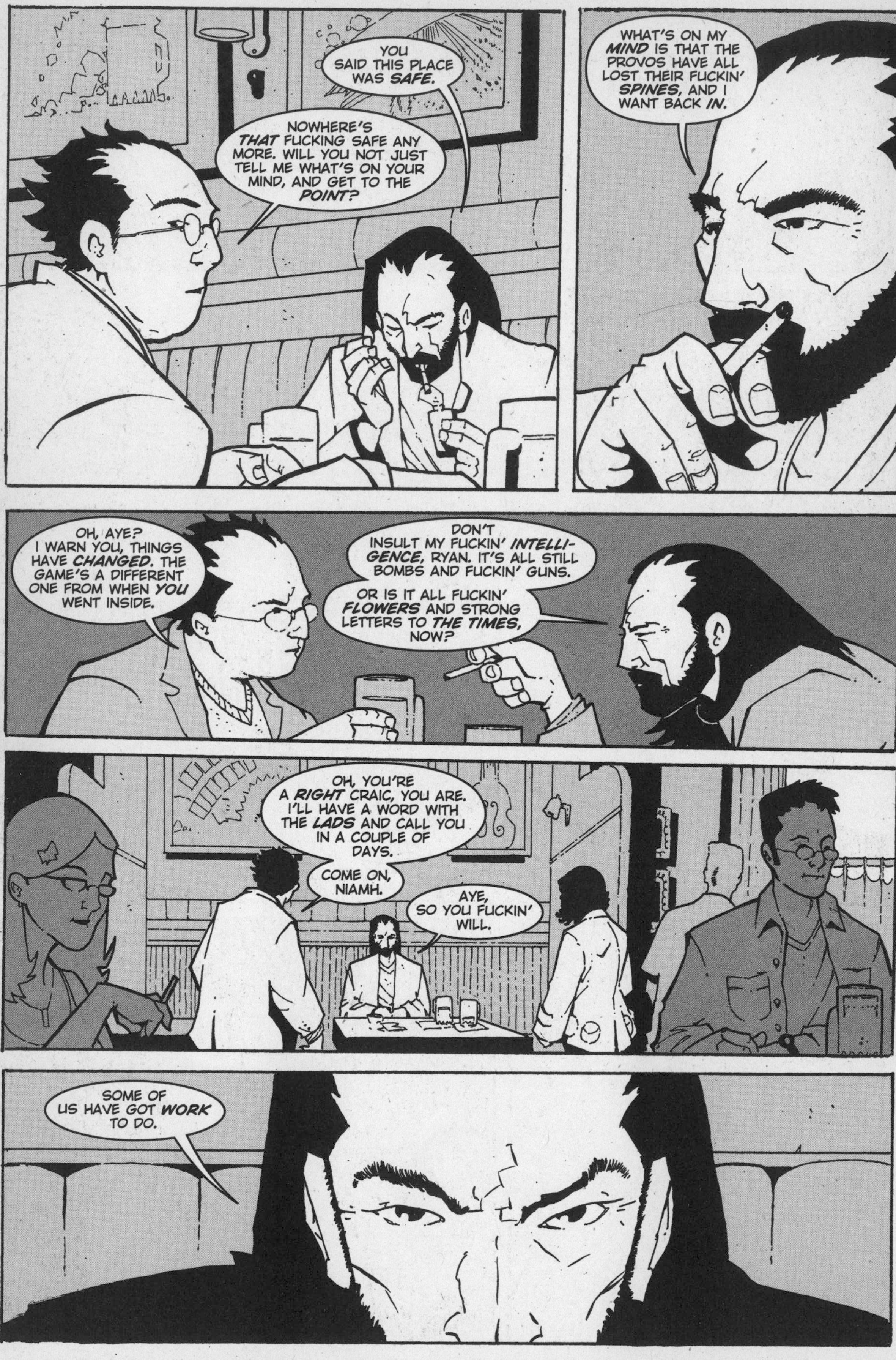
YOU SAID THIS PLACE WAS *SAFE.*
NOWHERE'S *THAT* FUCKING SAFE ANY MORE. WILL YOU NOT JUST TELL ME WHAT'S ON YOUR MIND, AND GET TO THE *POINT?*
WHAT'S ON MY *MIND* IS THAT THE PROVOS HAVE ALL LOST THEIR FUCKIN' *SPINES,* AND I WANT BACK *IN.*
OH, AYE? I WARN YOU, THINGS HAVE *CHANGED.* THE GAME'S A DIFFERENT ONE FROM WHEN *YOU* WENT INSIDE.
DON'T INSULT MY FUCKIN' *INTELLI-GENCE,* RYAN. IT'S ALL STILL BOMBS AND FUCKIN' GUNS.
OR IS IT ALL FUCKIN' *FLOWERS* AND STRONG LETTERS TO *THE TIMES,* NOW?
OH, YOU'RE A *RIGHT* CRAIC, YOU ARE. I'LL HAVE A WORD WITH THE *LADS* AND CALL YOU IN A COUPLE OF DAYS.
COME ON, NIAMH.
AYE, SO YOU FUCKIN' WILL.
SOME OF US HAVE GOT *WORK* TO DO.

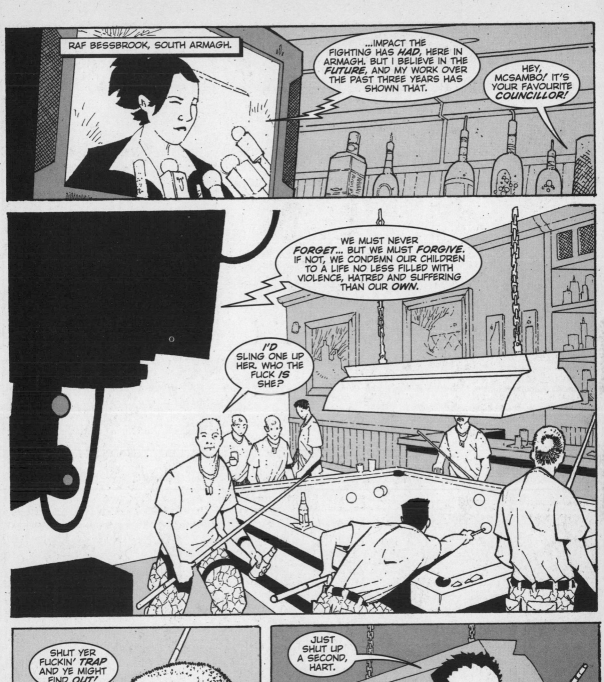

RAF BESSBROOK, SOUTH ARMAGH.

...IMPACT THE FIGHTING HAS *HAD*, HERE IN ARMAGH. BUT I BELIEVE IN THE *FUTURE*, AND MY WORK OVER THE PAST THREE YEARS HAS SHOWN THAT.

HEY, MCSAMBO! IT'S YOUR FAVOURITE *COUNCILLOR!*

WE MUST NEVER *FORGET...* BUT WE MUST *FORGIVE.* IF NOT, WE CONDEMN OUR CHILDREN TO A LIFE NO LESS FILLED WITH VIOLENCE, HATRED AND SUFFERING THAN OUR *OWN.*

I'D SLING ONE UP HER. WHO THE FUCK *IS* SHE?

SHUT YER FUCKIN' *TRAP* AND YE MIGHT FIND *OUT!*

OOH, GET *SAMBO.*

JUST SHUT UP A SECOND, HART.

I BELIEVE IRELAND IS STRONG ENOUGH TO *FACE* THESE CHALLENGES... AND STRONG ENOUGH TO FACE THEM *ALONE.*

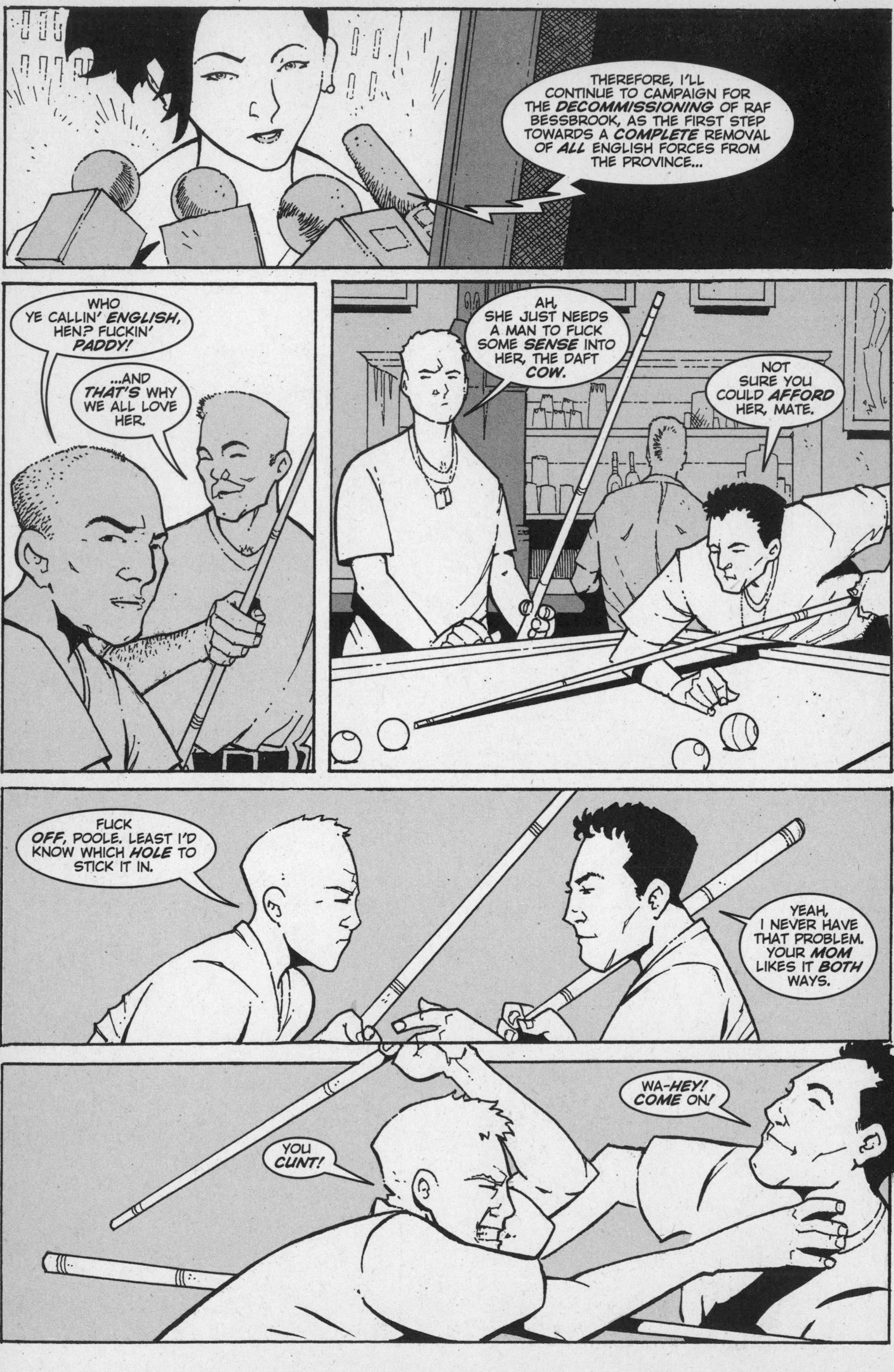
THEREFORE, I'LL CONTINUE TO CAMPAIGN FOR THE DECOMMISSIONING OF RAF BESSBROOK, AS THE FIRST STEP TOWARDS A COMPLETE REMOVAL OF ALL ENGLISH FORCES FROM THE PROVINCE...
WHO YE CALLIN' ENGLISH, HEN? FUCKIN' PADDY!
...AND THAT'S WHY WE ALL LOVE HER.
AH, SHE JUST NEEDS A MAN TO FUCK SOME SENSE INTO HER, THE DAFT COW.
NOT SURE YOU COULD AFFORD HER, MATE.
FUCK OFF, POOLE. LEAST I'D KNOW WHICH HOLE TO STICK IT IN.
YEAH, I NEVER HAVE THAT PROBLEM. YOUR MOM LIKES IT BOTH WAYS.
YOU CUNT!
WA-HEY! COME ON!

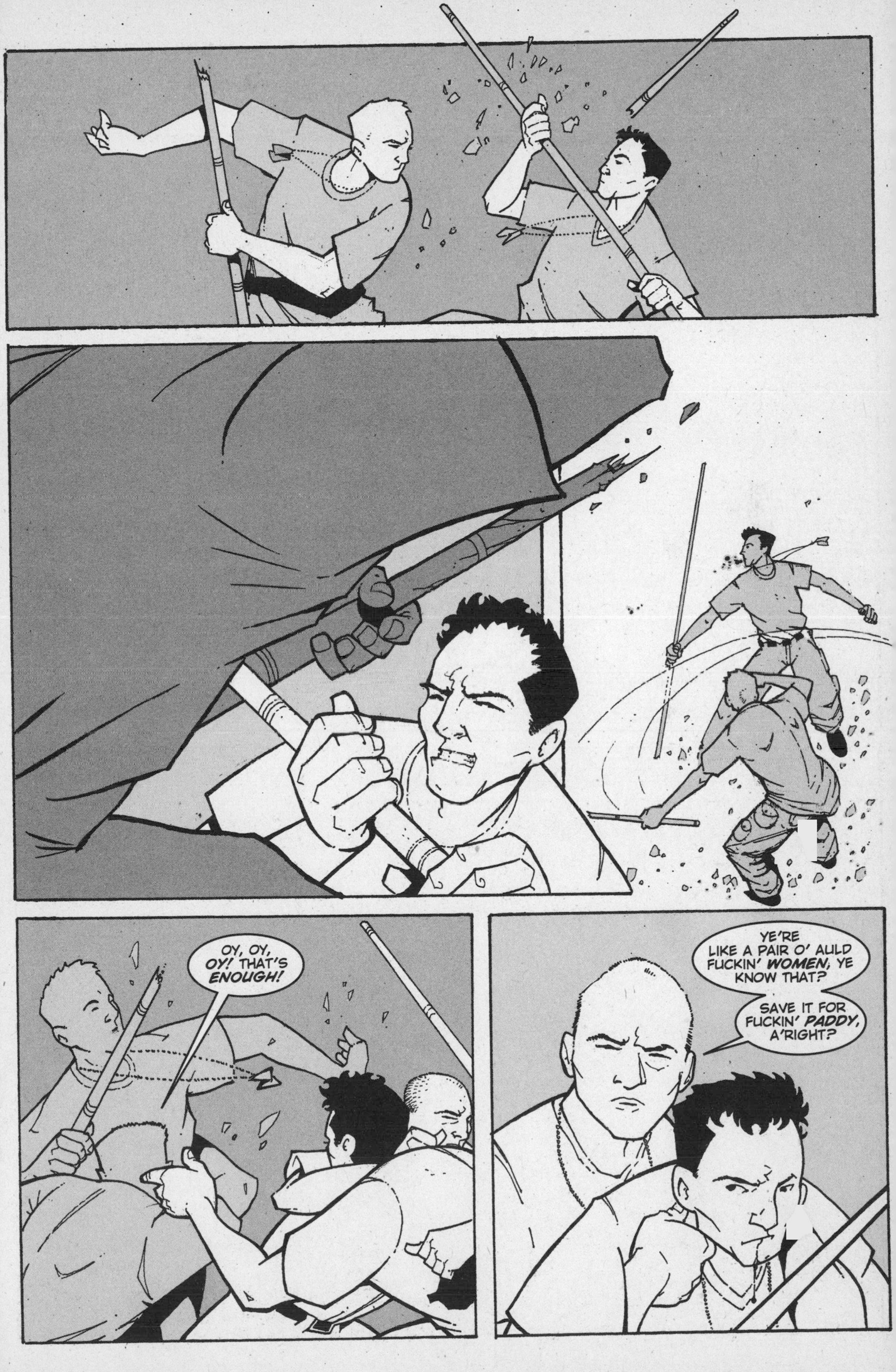
OY, OY, OY! THAT'S ENOUGH!
YE'RE LIKE A PAIR O' AULD FUCKIN' WOMEN, YE KNOW THAT?
SAVE IT FOR FUCKIN' PADDY, A'RIGHT?

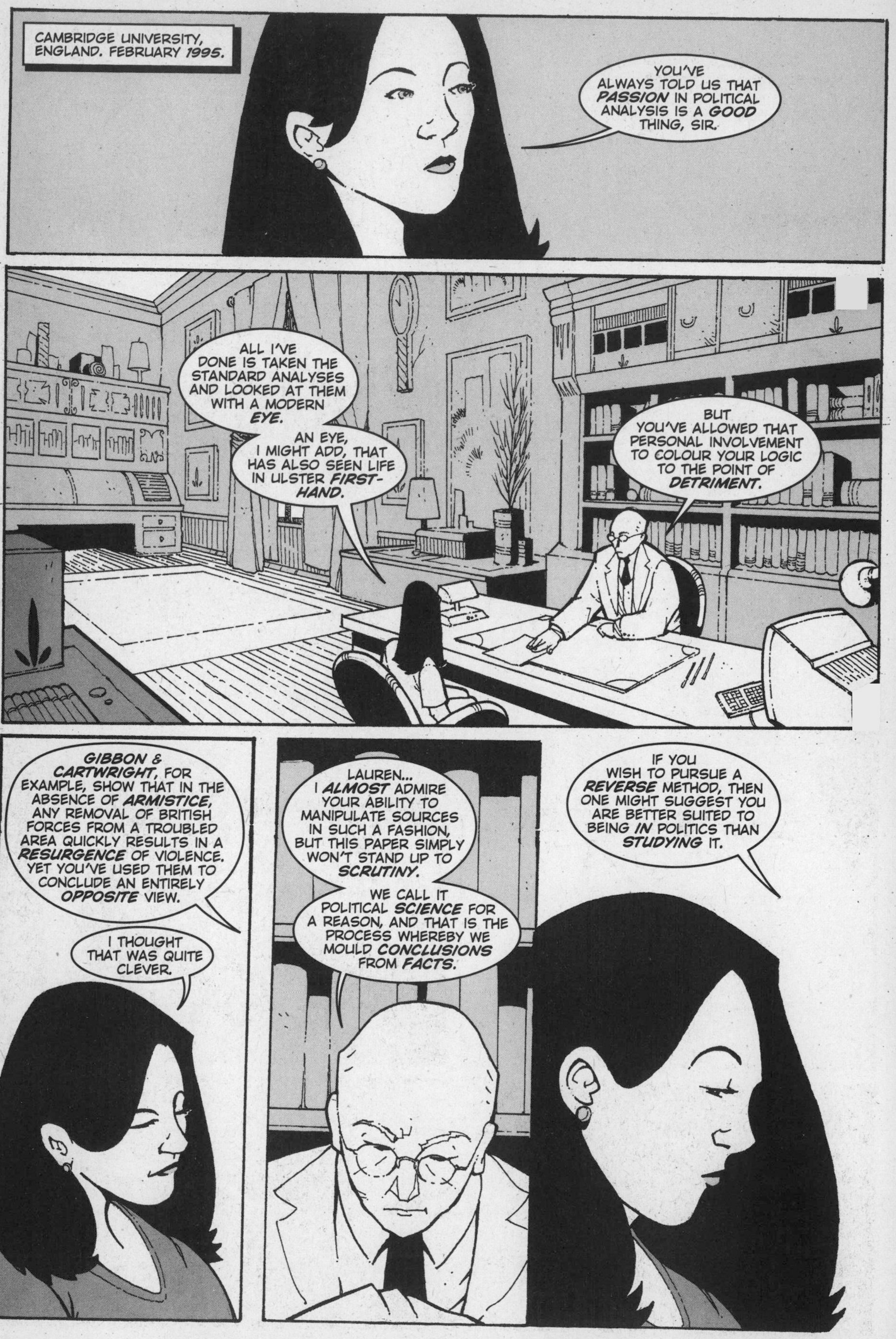
CAMBRIDGE UNIVERSITY, ENGLAND. FEBRUARY 1995.
YOU'VE ALWAYS TOLD US THAT PASSION IN POLITICAL ANALYSIS IS A GOOD THING, SIR.
ALL I'VE DONE IS TAKEN THE STANDARD ANALYSES AND LOOKED AT THEM WITH A MODERN EYE.
AN EYE, I MIGHT ADD, THAT HAS ALSO SEEN LIFE IN ULSTER FIRST-HAND.
BUT YOU'VE ALLOWED THAT PERSONAL INVOLVEMENT TO COLOUR YOUR LOGIC TO THE POINT OF DETRIMENT.
GIBBON & CARTWRIGHT, FOR EXAMPLE, SHOW THAT IN THE ABSENCE OF ARMISTICE, ANY REMOVAL OF BRITISH FORCES FROM A TROUBLED AREA QUICKLY RESULTS IN A RESURGENCE OF VIOLENCE. YET YOU'VE USED THEM TO CONCLUDE AN ENTIRELY OPPOSITE VIEW.
I THOUGHT THAT WAS QUITE CLEVER.
LAUREN... I ALMOST ADMIRE YOUR ABILITY TO MANIPULATE SOURCES IN SUCH A FASHION, BUT THIS PAPER SIMPLY WON'T STAND UP TO SCRUTINY.
WE CALL IT POLITICAL SCIENCE FOR A REASON, AND THAT IS THE PROCESS WHEREBY WE MOULD CONCLUSIONS FROM FACTS.
IF YOU WISH TO PURSUE A REVERSE METHOD, THEN ONE MIGHT SUGGEST YOU ARE BETTER SUITED TO BEING IN POLITICS THAN STUDYING IT.

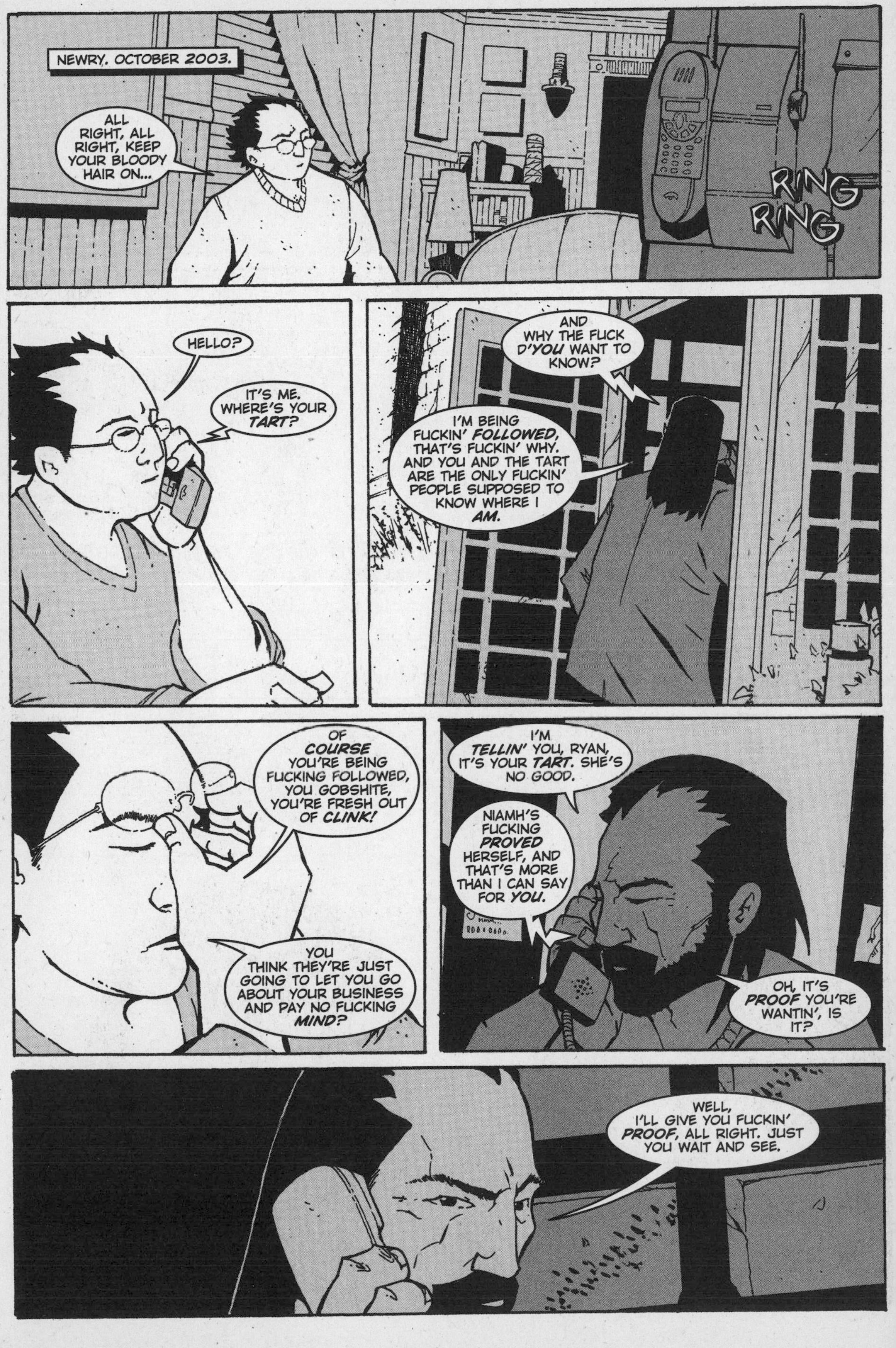
NEWRY. OCTOBER 2003.
ALL RIGHT, ALL RIGHT, KEEP YOUR BLOODY HAIR ON...
RING RING
HELLO?
IT'S ME. WHERE'S YOUR TART?
AND WHY THE FUCK D'YOU WANT TO KNOW?
I'M BEING FUCKIN' FOLLOWED, THAT'S FUCKIN' WHY. AND YOU AND THE TART ARE THE ONLY FUCKIN' PEOPLE SUPPOSED TO KNOW WHERE I AM.
OF COURSE YOU'RE BEING FUCKING FOLLOWED, YOU GOBSHITE, YOU'RE FRESH OUT OF CLINK!
YOU THINK THEY'RE JUST GOING TO LET YOU GO ABOUT YOUR BUSINESS AND PAY NO FUCKING MIND?
I'M TELLIN' YOU, RYAN, IT'S YOUR TART. SHE'S NO GOOD.
NIAMH'S FUCKING PROVED HERSELF, AND THAT'S MORE THAN I CAN SAY FOR YOU.
OH, IT'S PROOF YOU'RE WANTIN', IS IT?
WELL, I'LL GIVE YOU FUCKIN' PROOF, ALL RIGHT. JUST YOU WAIT AND SEE.

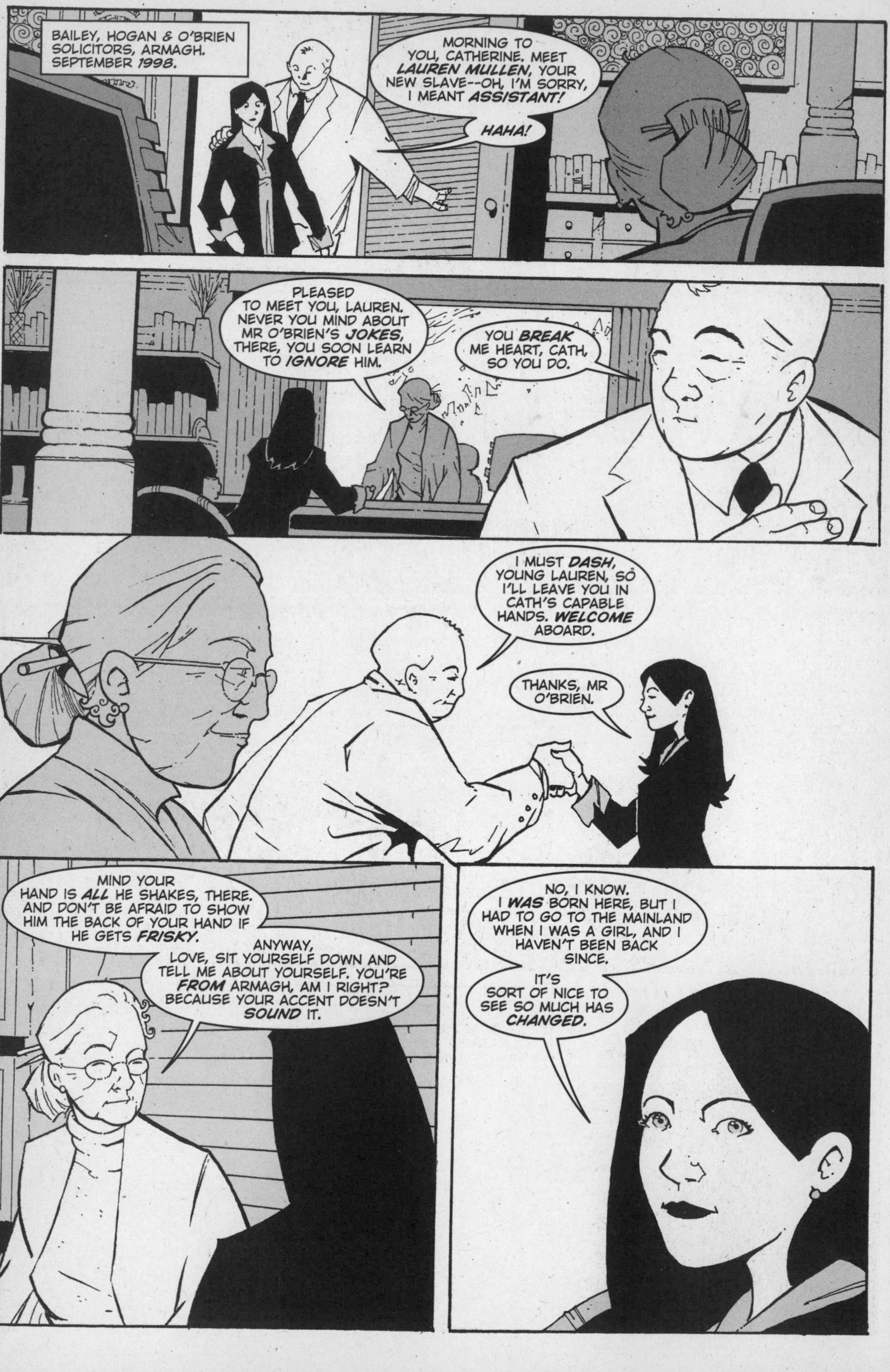
BAILEY, HOGAN & O'BRIEN SOLICITORS, ARMAGH. SEPTEMBER 1998.
MORNING TO YOU, CATHERINE. MEET LAUREN MULLEN, YOUR NEW SLAVE--OH, I'M SORRY, I MEANT ASSISTANT!
HAHA!
PLEASED TO MEET YOU, LAUREN. NEVER YOU MIND ABOUT MR O'BRIEN'S JOKES, THERE, YOU SOON LEARN TO IGNORE HIM.
YOU BREAK ME HEART, CATH, SO YOU DO.
I MUST DASH, YOUNG LAUREN, SO I'LL LEAVE YOU IN CATH'S CAPABLE HANDS. WELCOME ABOARD.
THANKS, MR O'BRIEN.
MIND YOUR HAND IS ALL HE SHAKES, THERE. AND DON'T BE AFRAID TO SHOW HIM THE BACK OF YOUR HAND IF HE GETS FRISKY.
ANYWAY, LOVE, SIT YOURSELF DOWN AND TELL ME ABOUT YOURSELF. YOU'RE FROM ARMAGH, AM I RIGHT? BECAUSE YOUR ACCENT DOESN'T SOUND IT.
NO, I KNOW. I WAS BORN HERE, BUT I HAD TO GO TO THE MAINLAND WHEN I WAS A GIRL, AND I HAVEN'T BEEN BACK SINCE.
IT'S SORT OF NICE TO SEE SO MUCH HAS CHANGED.

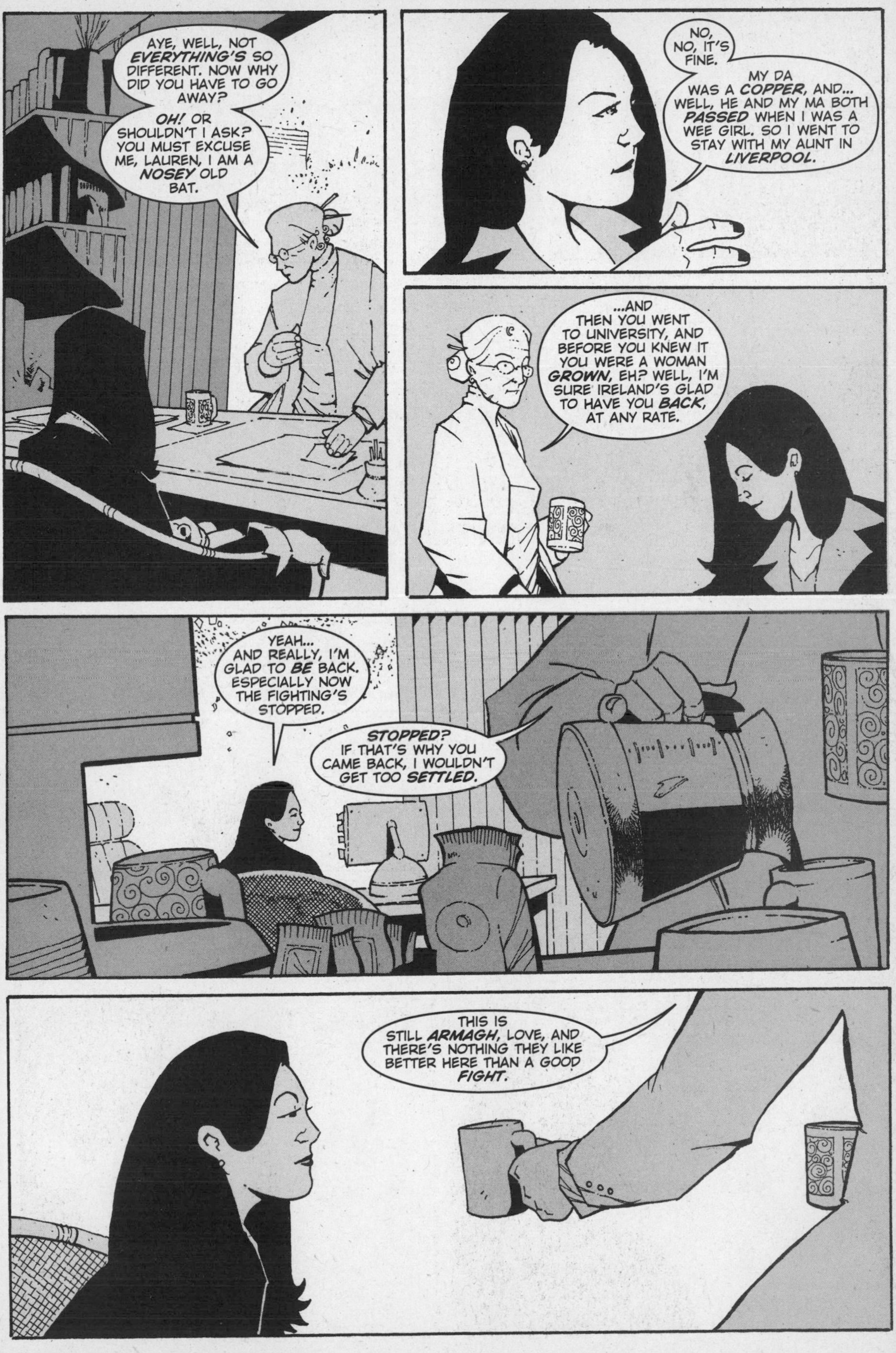

AYE, WELL, NOT EVERYTHING'S SO DIFFERENT. NOW WHY DID YOU HAVE TO GO AWAY?
OH! OR SHOULDN'T I ASK? YOU MUST EXCUSE ME, LAUREN, I AM A NOSEY OLD BAT.
NO, NO, IT'S FINE.
MY DA WAS A COPPER, AND... WELL, HE AND MY MA BOTH PASSED WHEN I WAS A WEE GIRL. SO I WENT TO STAY WITH MY AUNT IN LIVERPOOL.
...AND THEN YOU WENT TO UNIVERSITY, AND BEFORE YOU KNEW IT YOU WERE A WOMAN GROWN, EH? WELL, I'M SURE IRELAND'S GLAD TO HAVE YOU BACK, AT ANY RATE.
YEAH... AND REALLY, I'M GLAD TO BE BACK. ESPECIALLY NOW THE FIGHTING'S STOPPED.
STOPPED? IF THAT'S WHY YOU CAME BACK, I WOULDN'T GET TOO SETTLED.
THIS IS STILL ARMAGH, LOVE, AND THERE'S NOTHING THEY LIKE BETTER HERE THAN A GOOD FIGHT.

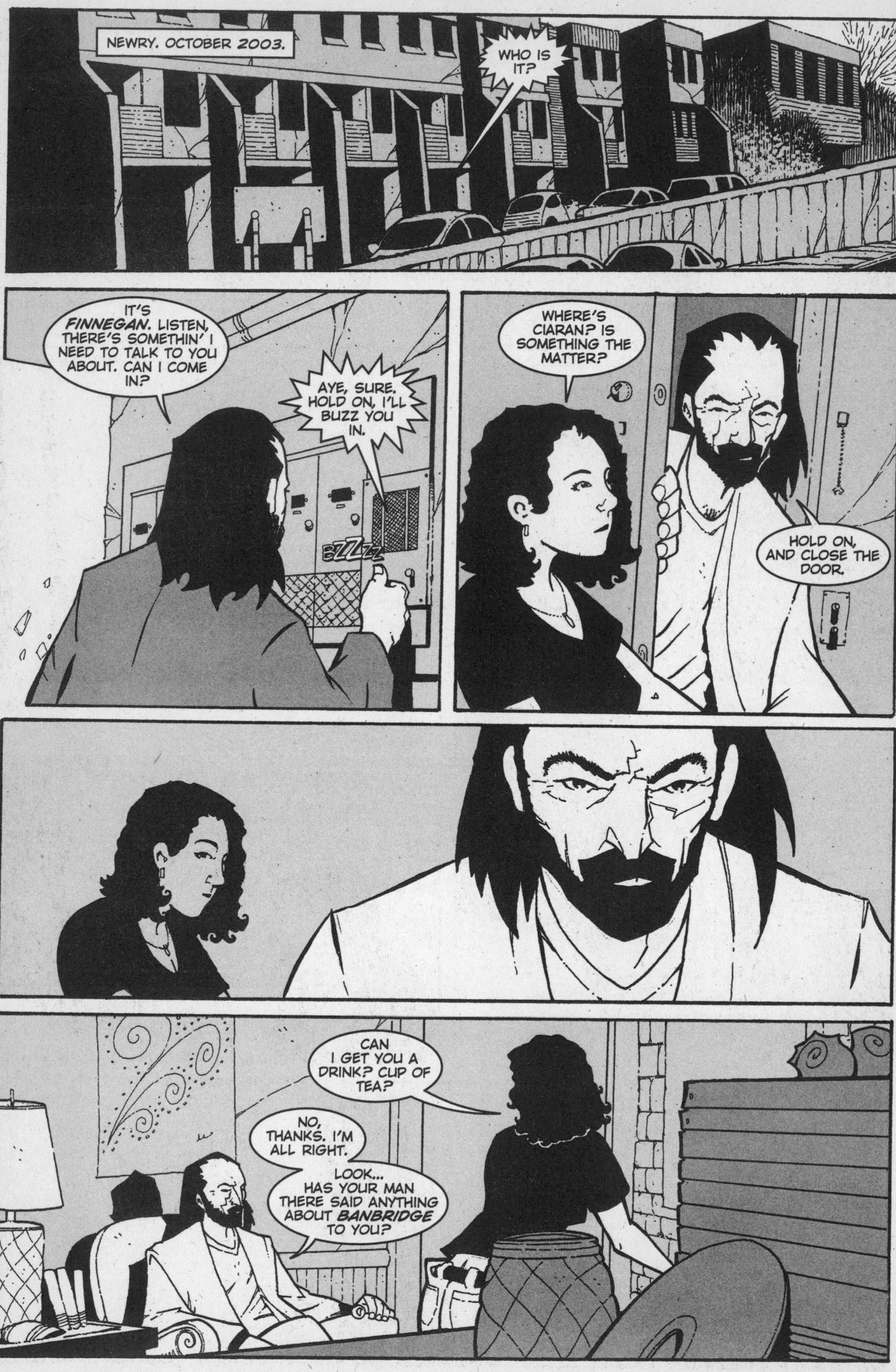

NEWRY. OCTOBER 2003.
WHO IS IT?
IT'S FINNEGAN. LISTEN, THERE'S SOMETHIN' I NEED TO TALK TO YOU ABOUT. CAN I COME IN?
AYE, SURE. HOLD ON, I'LL BUZZ YOU IN.
BZZZZ
WHERE'S CIARAN? IS SOMETHING THE MATTER?
HOLD ON, AND CLOSE THE DOOR.
CAN I GET YOU A DRINK? CUP OF TEA?
NO, THANKS. I'M ALL RIGHT.
LOOK... HAS YOUR MAN THERE SAID ANYTHING ABOUT BANBRIDGE TO YOU?

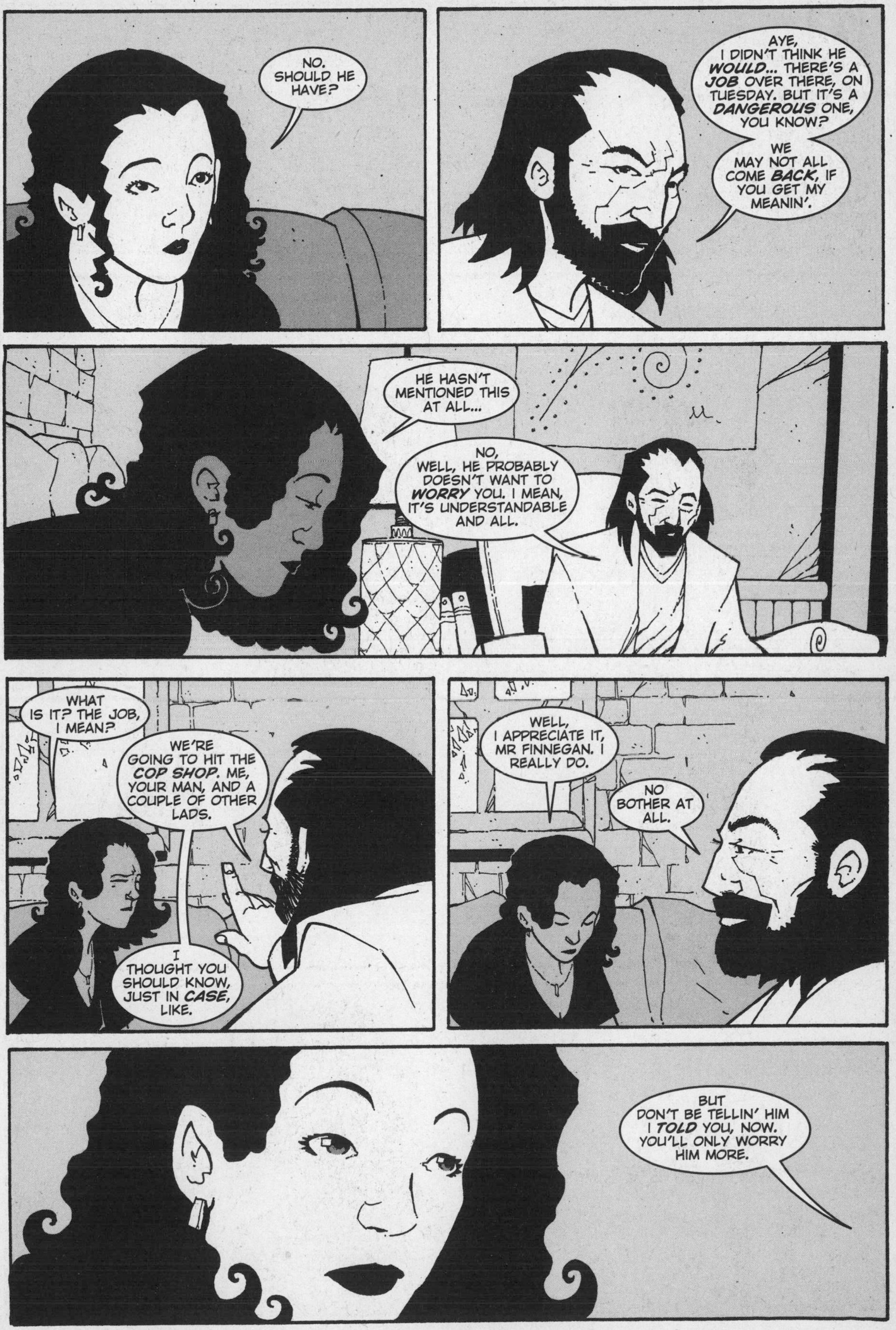
NO. SHOULD HE HAVE?
AYE, I DIDN'T THINK HE WOULD... THERE'S A JOB OVER THERE, ON TUESDAY. BUT IT'S A DANGEROUS ONE, YOU KNOW?
WE MAY NOT ALL COME BACK, IF YOU GET MY MEANIN'.
HE HASN'T MENTIONED THIS AT ALL...
NO, WELL, HE PROBABLY DOESN'T WANT TO WORRY YOU. I MEAN, IT'S UNDERSTANDABLE AND ALL.
WHAT IS IT? THE JOB, I MEAN?
WE'RE GOING TO HIT THE COP SHOP. ME, YOUR MAN, AND A COUPLE OF OTHER LADS.
I THOUGHT YOU SHOULD KNOW, JUST IN CASE, LIKE.
WELL, I APPRECIATE IT, MR FINNEGAN. I REALLY DO.
NO BOTHER AT ALL.
BUT DON'T BE TELLIN' HIM I TOLD YOU, NOW. YOU'LL ONLY WORRY HIM MORE.

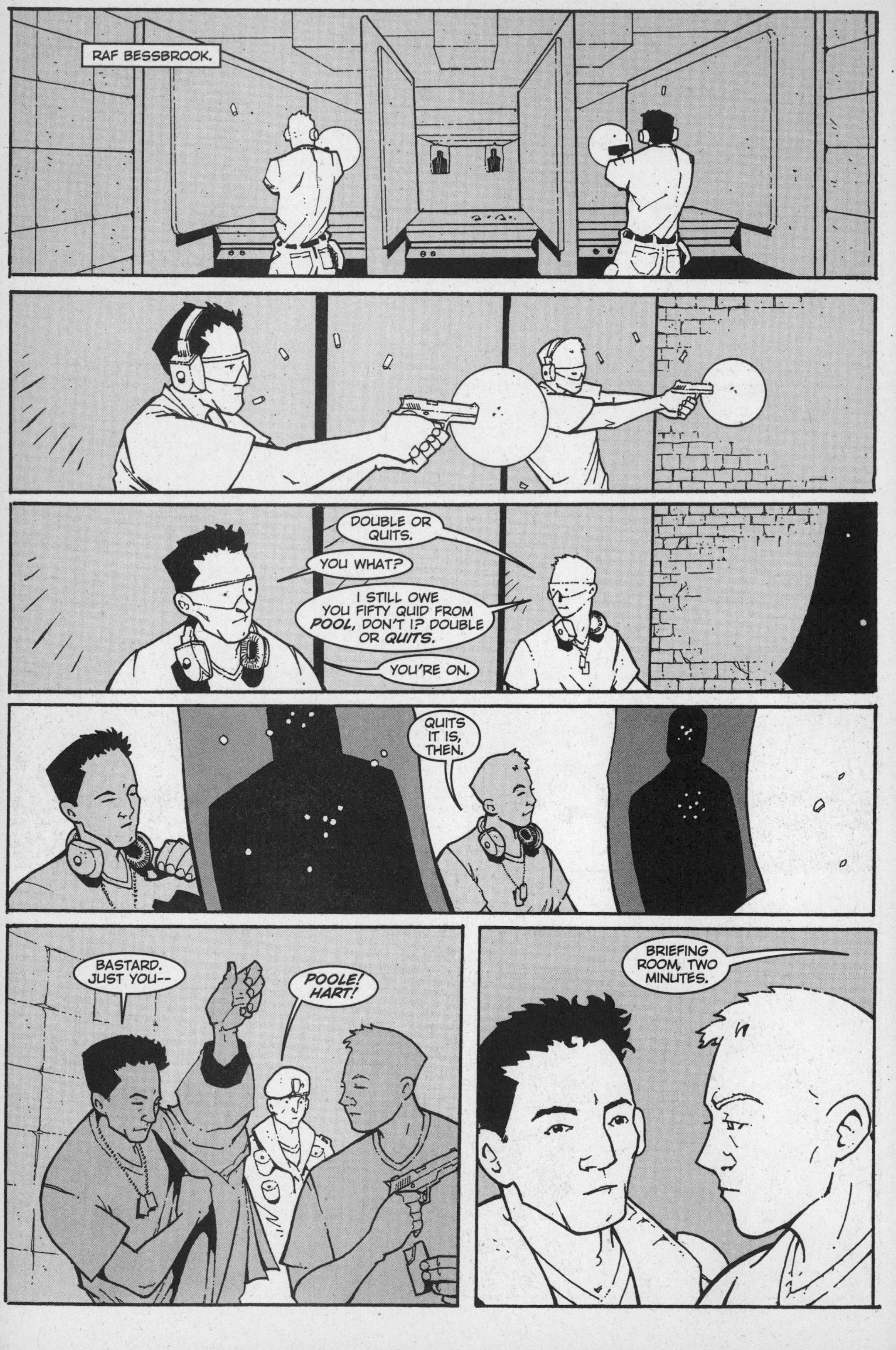
RAF BESSBROOK.
DOUBLE OR QUITS.
YOU WHAT?
I STILL OWE YOU FIFTY QUID FROM POOL, DON'T I? DOUBLE OR QUITS.
YOU'RE ON.
QUITS IT IS, THEN.
BASTARD. JUST YOU--
POOLE! HART!
BRIEFING ROOM, TWO MINUTES.

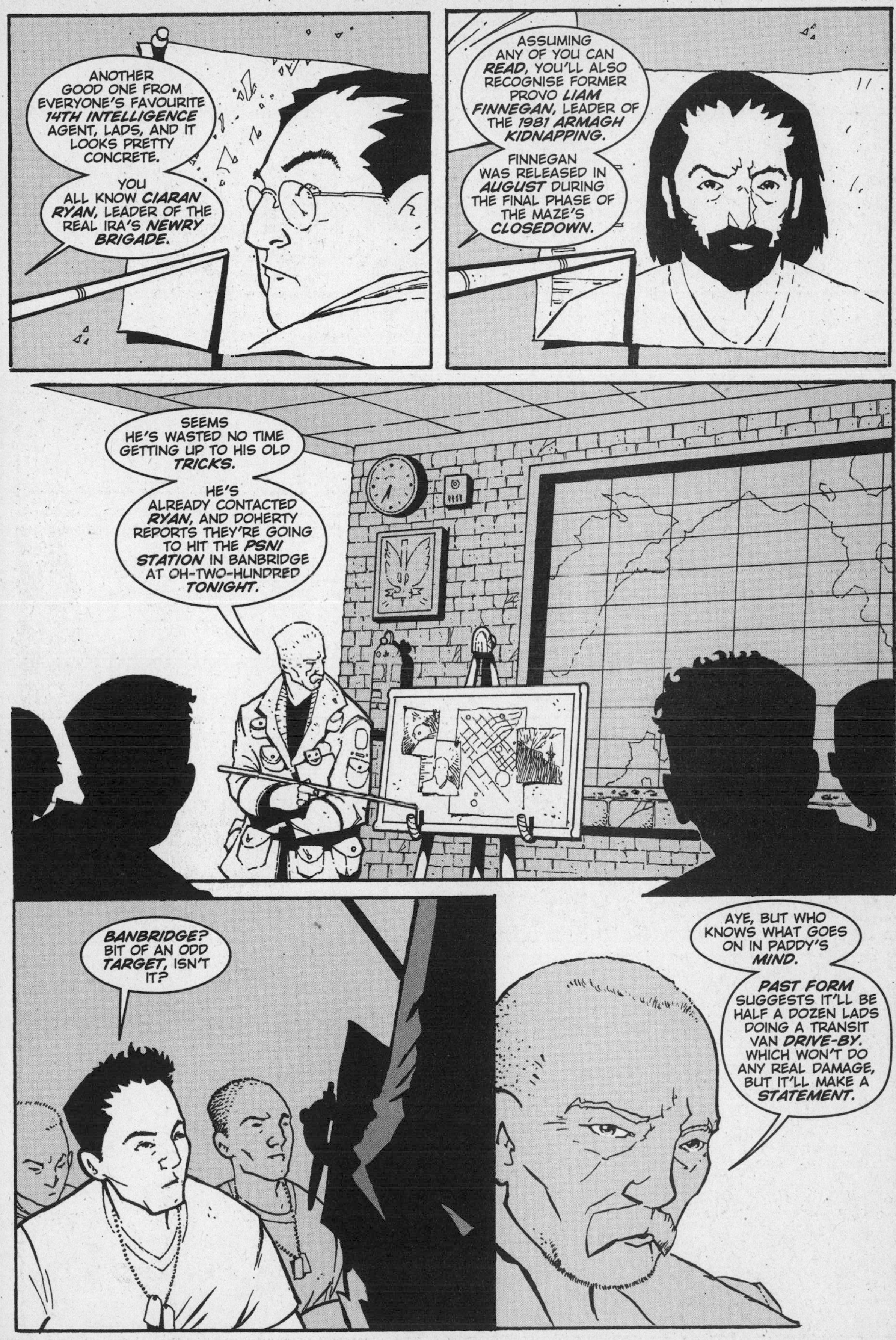
ANOTHER GOOD ONE FROM EVERYONE'S FAVOURITE 14TH INTELLIGENCE AGENT, LADS, AND IT LOOKS PRETTY CONCRETE.
YOU ALL KNOW CIARAN RYAN, LEADER OF THE REAL IRA'S NEWRY BRIGADE.
ASSUMING ANY OF YOU CAN READ, YOU'LL ALSO RECOGNISE FORMER PROVO LIAM FINNEGAN, LEADER OF THE 1981 ARMAGH KIDNAPPING.
FINNEGAN WAS RELEASED IN AUGUST DURING THE FINAL PHASE OF THE MAZE'S CLOSEDOWN.
SEEMS HE'S WASTED NO TIME GETTING UP TO HIS OLD TRICKS.
HE'S ALREADY CONTACTED RYAN, AND DOHERTY REPORTS THEY'RE GOING TO HIT THE PSNI STATION IN BANBRIDGE AT OH-TWO-HUNDRED TONIGHT.
BANBRIDGE? BIT OF AN ODD TARGET, ISN'T IT?
AYE, BUT WHO KNOWS WHAT GOES ON IN PADDY'S MIND.
PAST FORM SUGGESTS IT'LL BE HALF A DOZEN LADS DOING A TRANSIT VAN DRIVE-BY. WHICH WON'T DO ANY REAL DAMAGE, BUT IT'LL MAKE A STATEMENT.

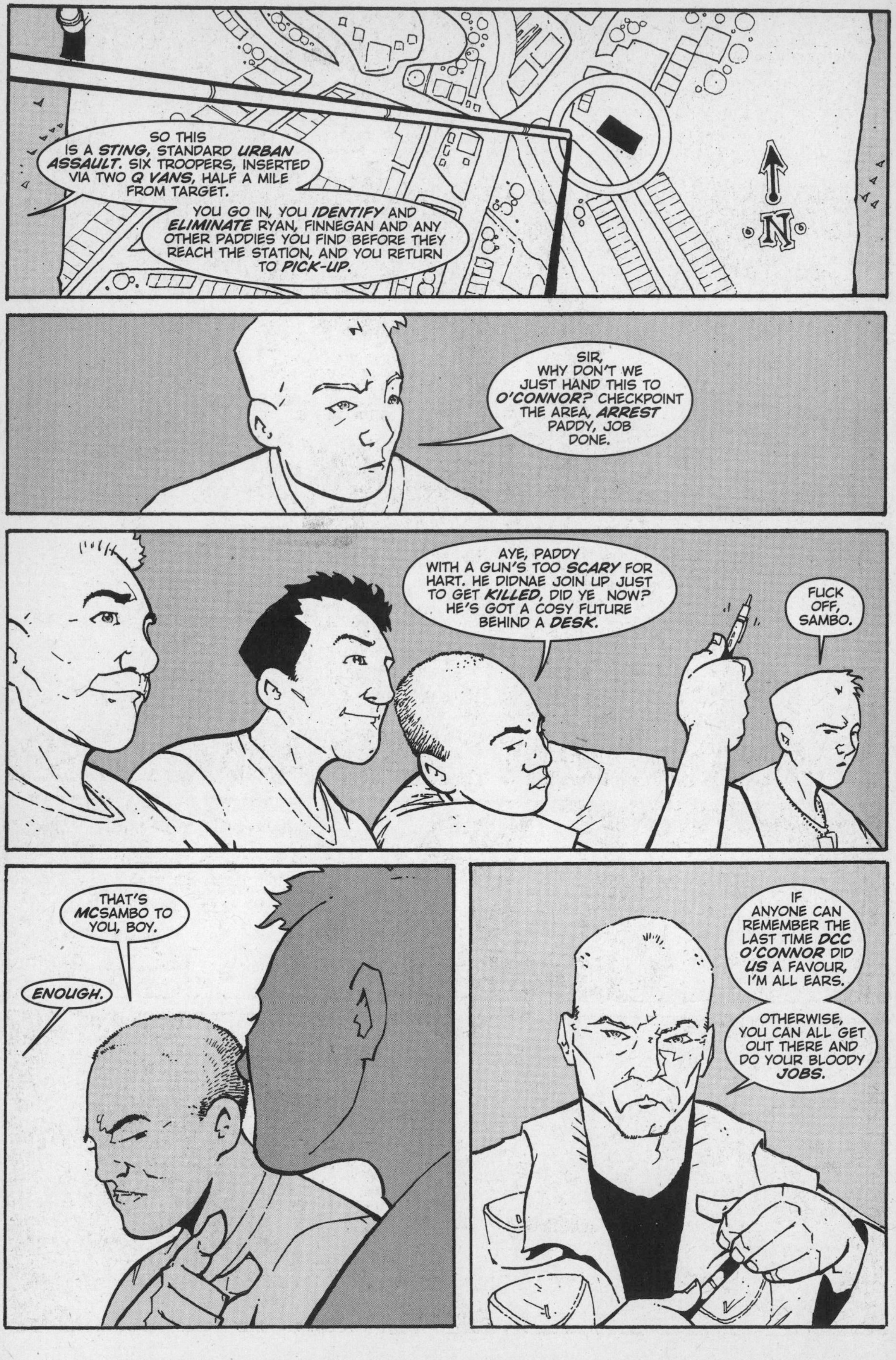
SO THIS IS A STING, STANDARD URBAN ASSAULT. SIX TROOPERS, INSERTED VIA TWO Q VANS, HALF A MILE FROM TARGET.
YOU GO IN, YOU IDENTIFY AND ELIMINATE RYAN, FINNEGAN AND ANY OTHER PADDIES YOU FIND BEFORE THEY REACH THE STATION, AND YOU RETURN TO PICK-UP.
N
SIR, WHY DON'T WE JUST HAND THIS TO O'CONNOR? CHECKPOINT THE AREA, ARREST PADDY, JOB DONE.
AYE, PADDY WITH A GUN'S TOO SCARY FOR HART. HE DIDNAE JOIN UP JUST TO GET KILLED, DID YE NOW? HE'S GOT A COSY FUTURE BEHIND A DESK.
FUCK OFF, SAMBO.
THAT'S MCSAMBO TO YOU, BOY.
ENOUGH.
IF ANYONE CAN REMEMBER THE LAST TIME DCC O'CONNOR DID US A FAVOUR, I'M ALL EARS.
OTHERWISE, YOU CAN ALL GET OUT THERE AND DO YOUR BLOODY JOBS.

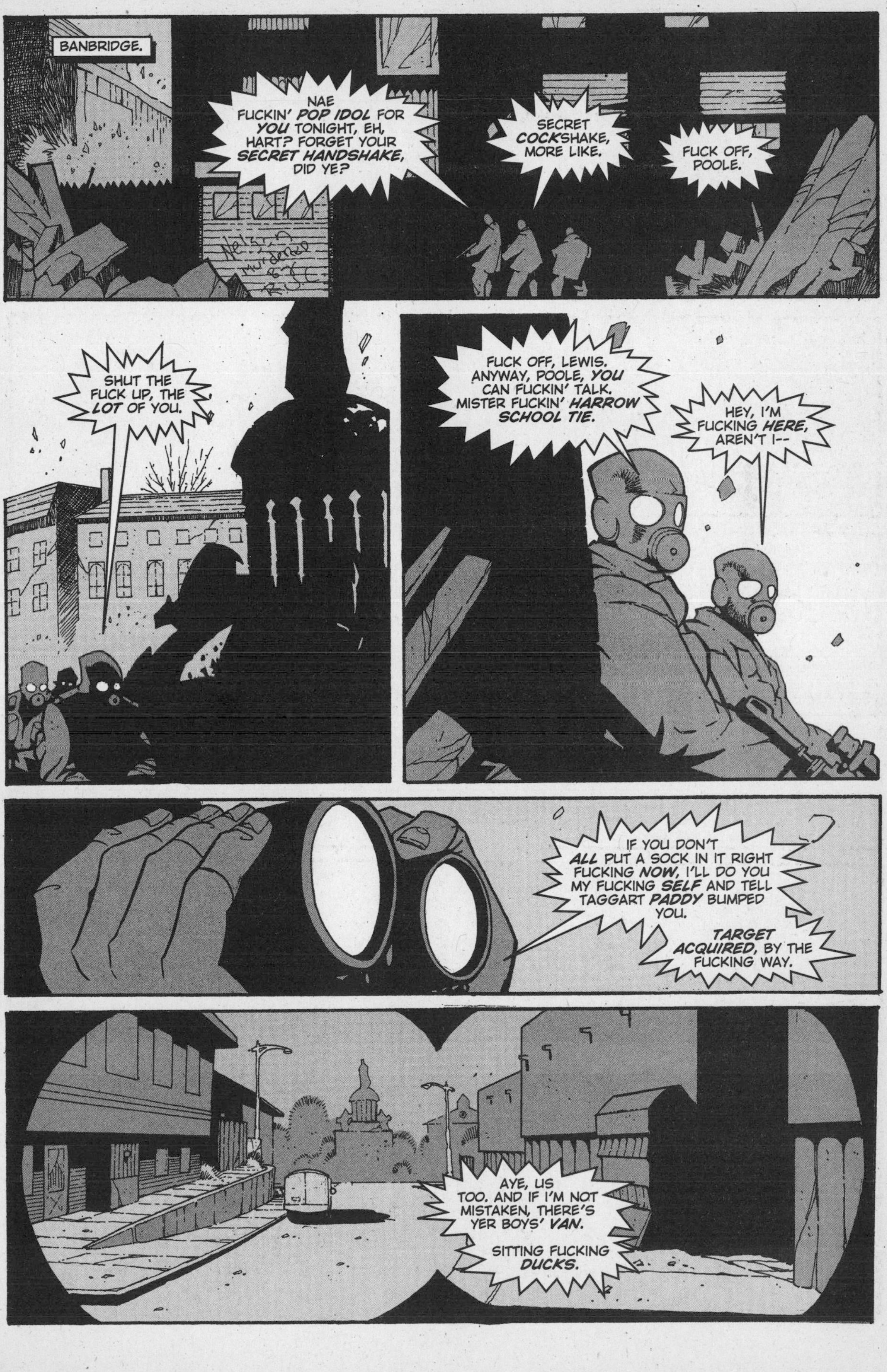
BANBRIDGE.
NAE FUCKIN' POP IDOL FOR YOU TONIGHT, EH, HART? FORGET YOUR SECRET HANDSHAKE, DID YE?
SECRET COCKSHAKE, MORE LIKE.
FUCK OFF, POOLE.
SHUT THE FUCK UP, THE LOT OF YOU.
FUCK OFF, LEWIS. ANYWAY, POOLE, YOU CAN FUCKIN' TALK. MISTER FUCKIN' HARROW SCHOOL TIE.
HEY, I'M FUCKING HERE, AREN'T I--
IF YOU DON'T ALL PUT A SOCK IN IT RIGHT FUCKING NOW, I'LL DO YOU MY FUCKING SELF AND TELL TAGGART PADDY BUMPED YOU.
TARGET ACQUIRED, BY THE FUCKING WAY.
AYE, US TOO. AND IF I'M NOT MISTAKEN, THERE'S YER BOYS' VAN.
SITTING FUCKING DUCKS.

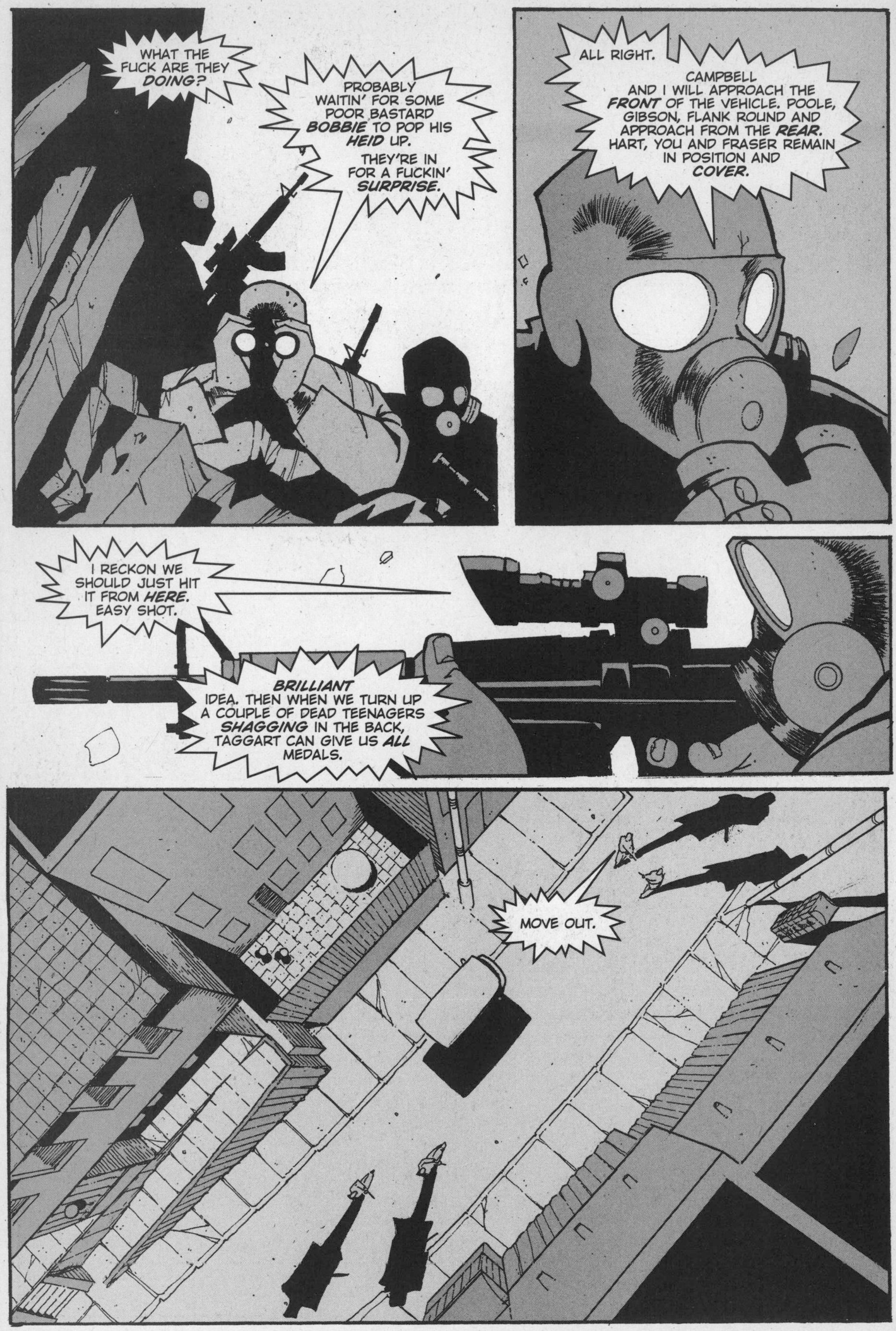
WHAT THE FUCK ARE THEY DOING?
PROBABLY WAITIN' FOR SOME POOR BASTARD BOBBIE TO POP HIS HEID UP.
THEY'RE IN FOR A FUCKIN' SURPRISE.
ALL RIGHT.
CAMPBELL AND I WILL APPROACH THE FRONT OF THE VEHICLE. POOLE, GIBSON, FLANK ROUND AND APPROACH FROM THE REAR. HART, YOU AND FRASER REMAIN IN POSITION AND COVER.
I RECKON WE SHOULD JUST HIT IT FROM HERE. EASY SHOT.
BRILLIANT IDEA. THEN WHEN WE TURN UP A COUPLE OF DEAD TEENAGERS SHAGGING IN THE BACK, TAGGART CAN GIVE US ALL MEDALS.
MOVE OUT.

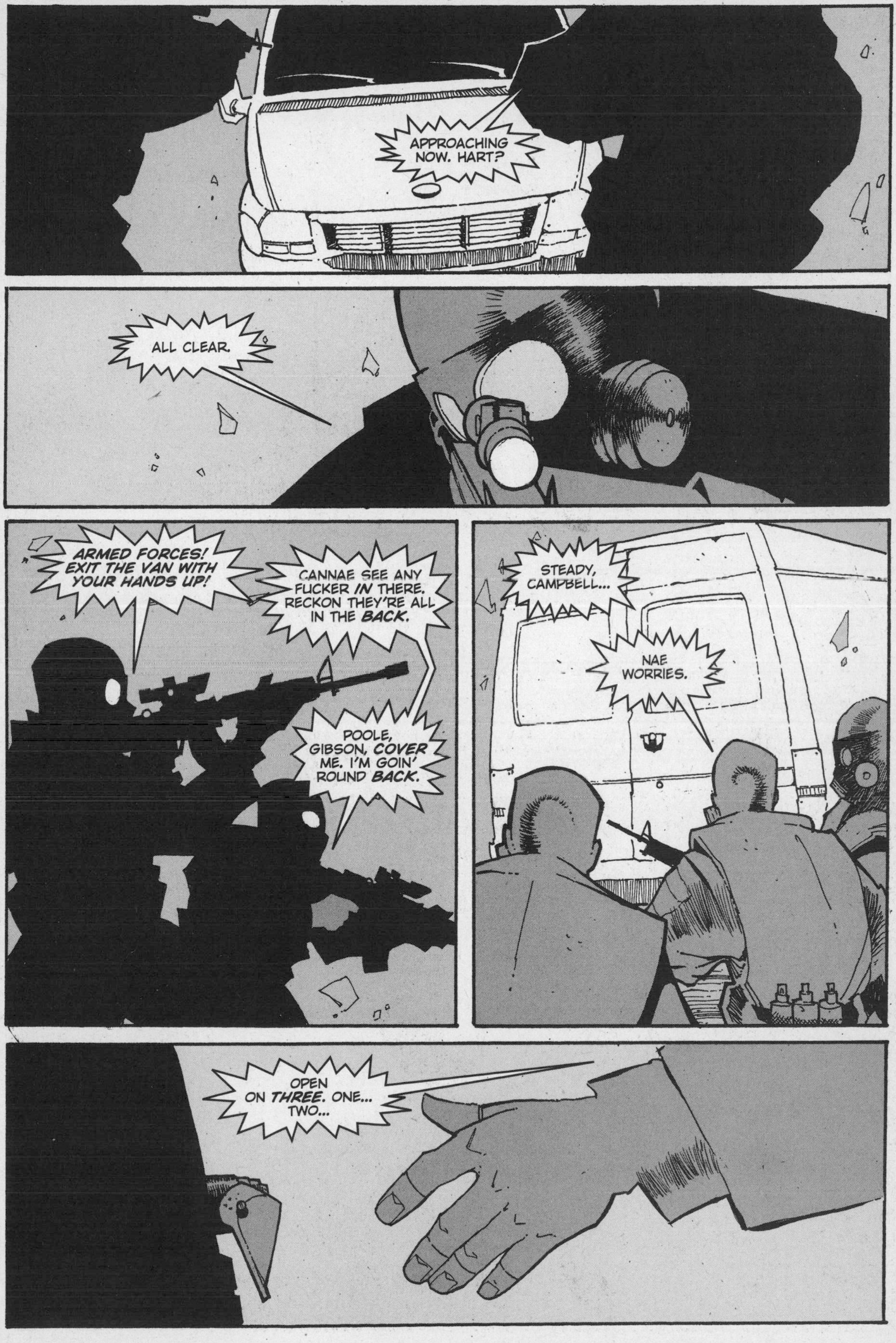
APPROACHING NOW. HART?
ALL CLEAR.
ARMED FORCES! EXIT THE VAN WITH YOUR HANDS UP!
CANNAE SEE ANY FUCKER IN THERE. RECKON THEY'RE ALL IN THE BACK.
POOLE, GIBSON, COVER ME. I'M GOIN' ROUND BACK.
STEADY, CAMPBELL...
NAE WORRIES.
OPEN ON THREE. ONE... TWO...

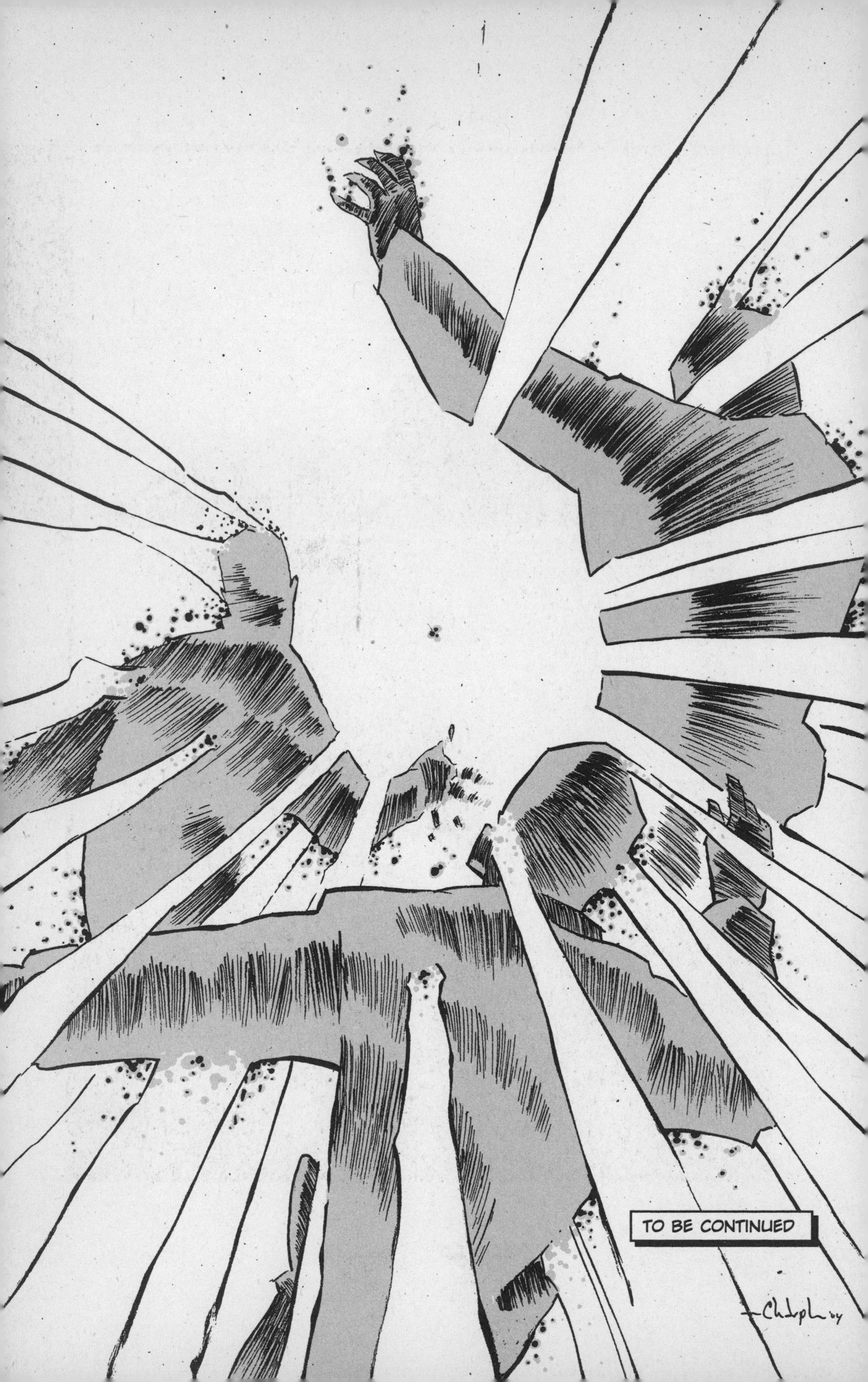
TO BE CONTINUED

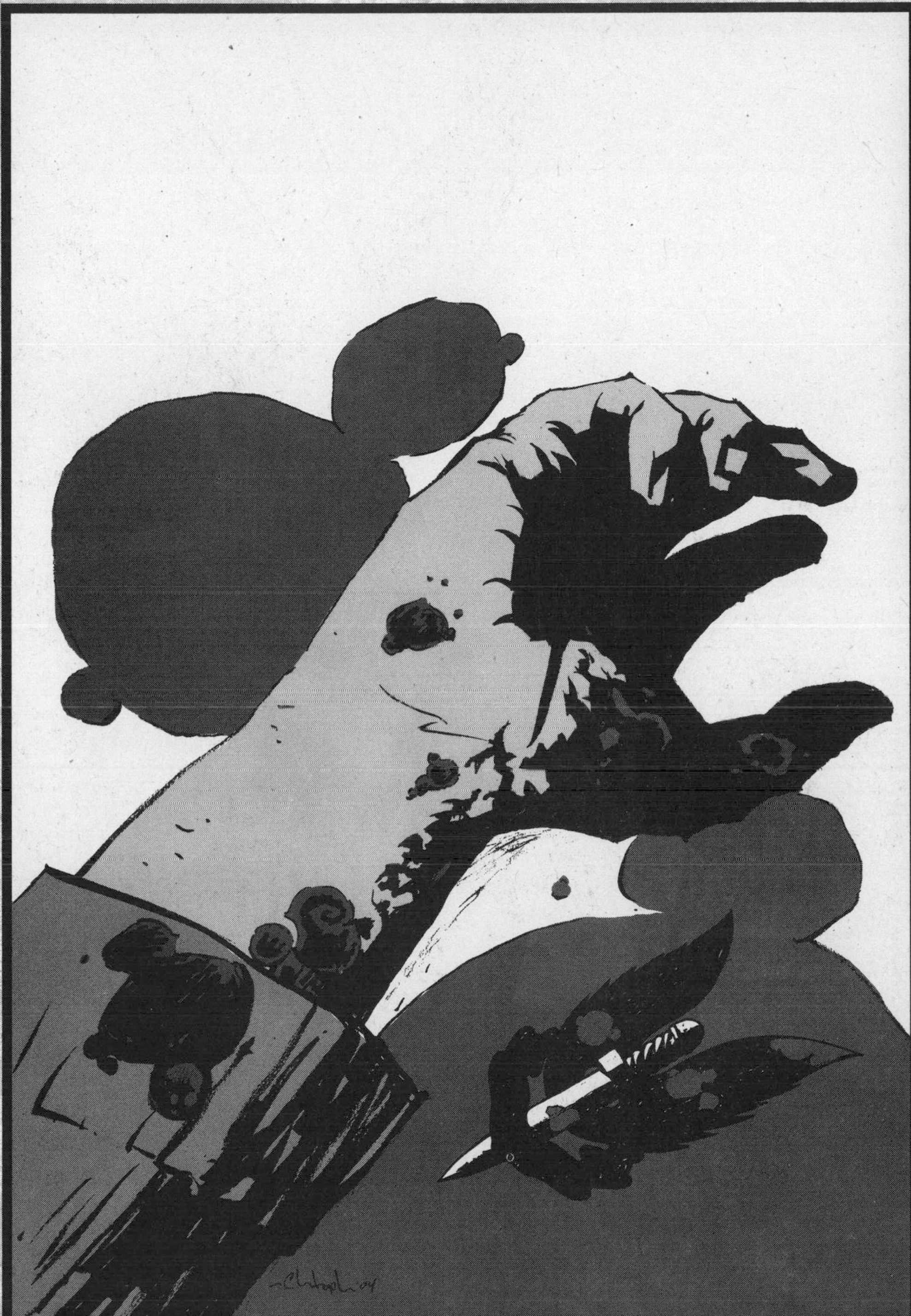

CHAPTER 2

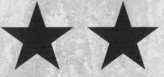

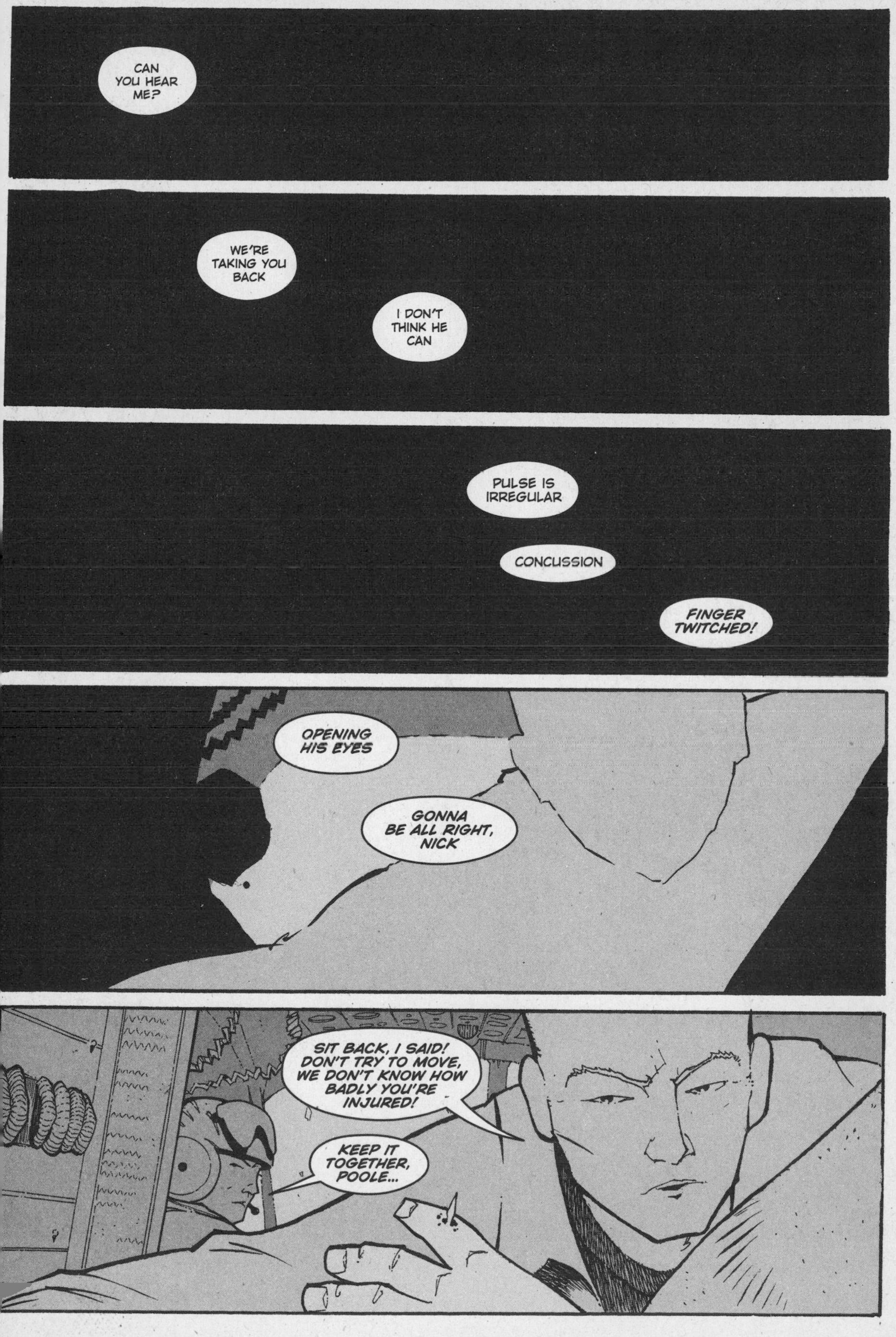
CAN YOU HEAR ME?
WE'RE TAKING YOU BACK
I DON'T THINK HE CAN
PULSE IS IRREGULAR
CONCUSSION
FINGER TWITCHED!
OPENING HIS EYES
GONNA BE ALL RIGHT, NICK
SIT BACK, I SAID! DON'T TRY TO MOVE, WE DON'T KNOW HOW BADLY YOU'RE INJURED!
KEEP IT TOGETHER, POOLE...

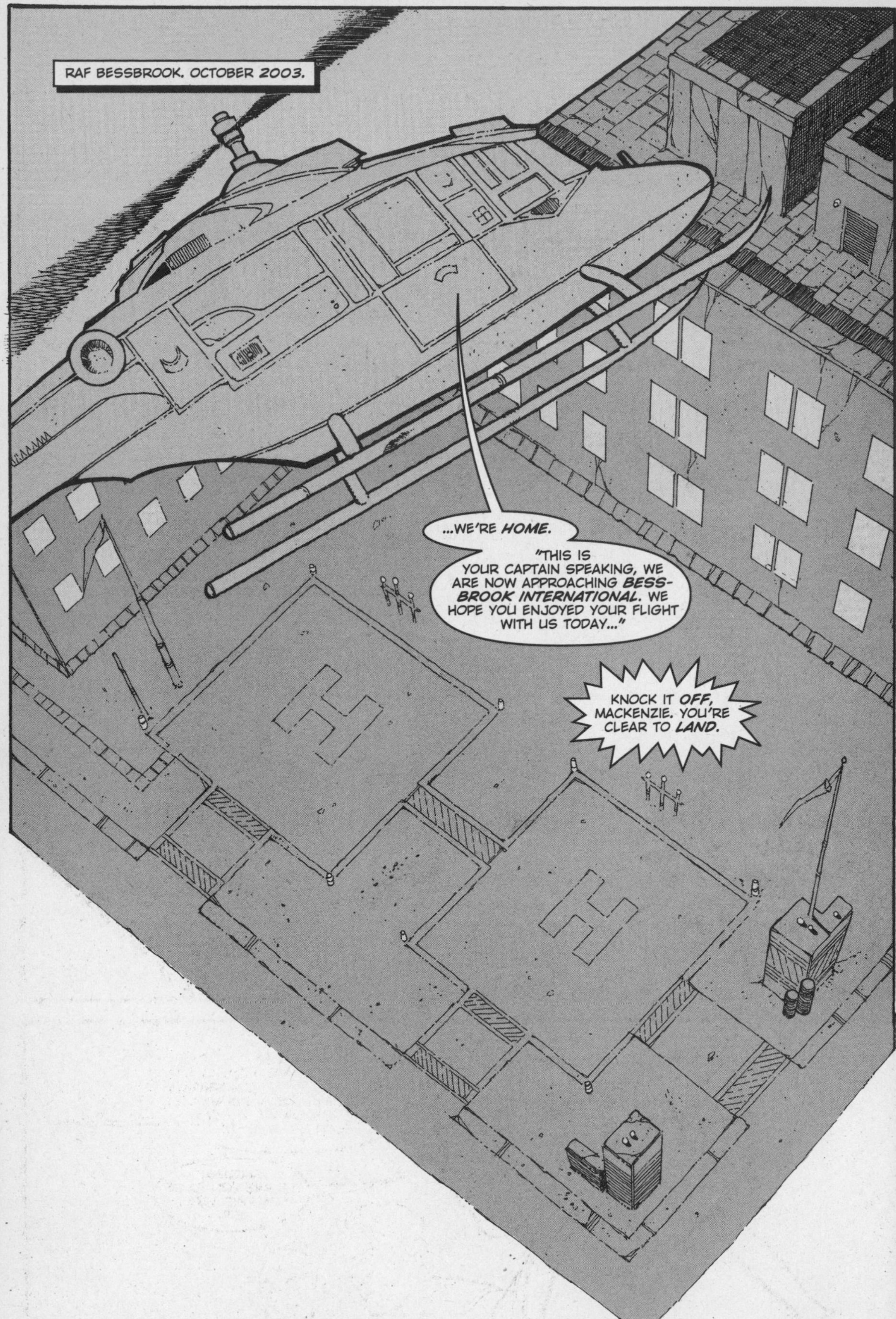

RAF BESSBROOK. OCTOBER 2003.
...WE'RE HOME.
"THIS IS YOUR CAPTAIN SPEAKING, WE ARE NOW APPROACHING BESS-BROOK INTERNATIONAL. WE HOPE YOU ENJOYED YOUR FLIGHT WITH US TODAY..."
KNOCK IT OFF, MACKENZIE. YOU'RE CLEAR TO LAND.

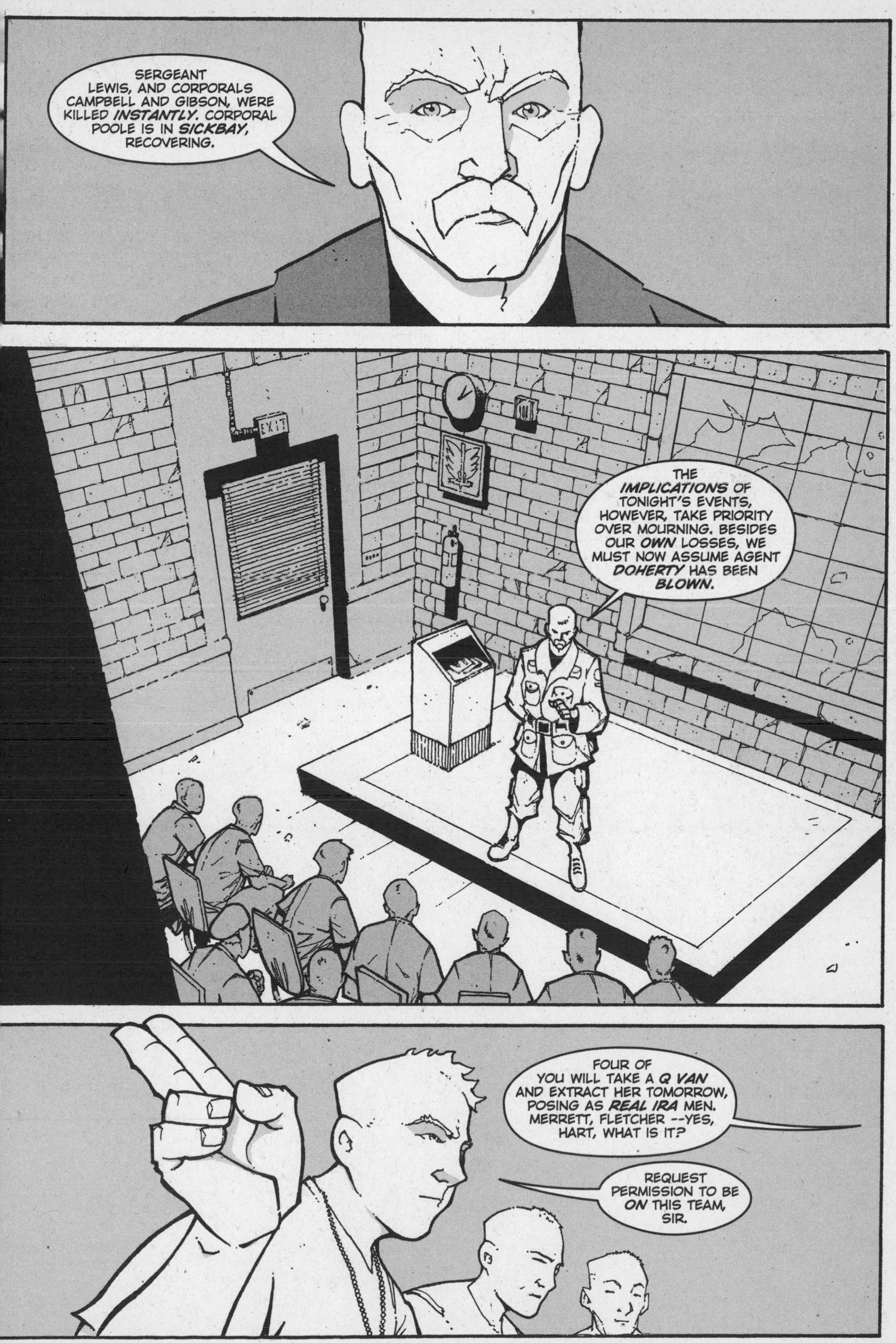
SERGEANT LEWIS, AND CORPORALS CAMPBELL AND GIBSON, WERE KILLED INSTANTLY. CORPORAL POOLE IS IN SICKBAY, RECOVERING.
EXIT
THE IMPLICATIONS OF TONIGHT'S EVENTS, HOWEVER, TAKE PRIORITY OVER MOURNING. BESIDES OUR OWN LOSSES, WE MUST NOW ASSUME AGENT DOHERTY HAS BEEN BLOWN.
FOUR OF YOU WILL TAKE A Q VAN AND EXTRACT HER TOMORROW, POSING AS REAL IRA MEN. MERRETT, FLETCHER --YES, HART, WHAT IS IT?
REQUEST PERMISSION TO BE ON THIS TEAM, SIR.

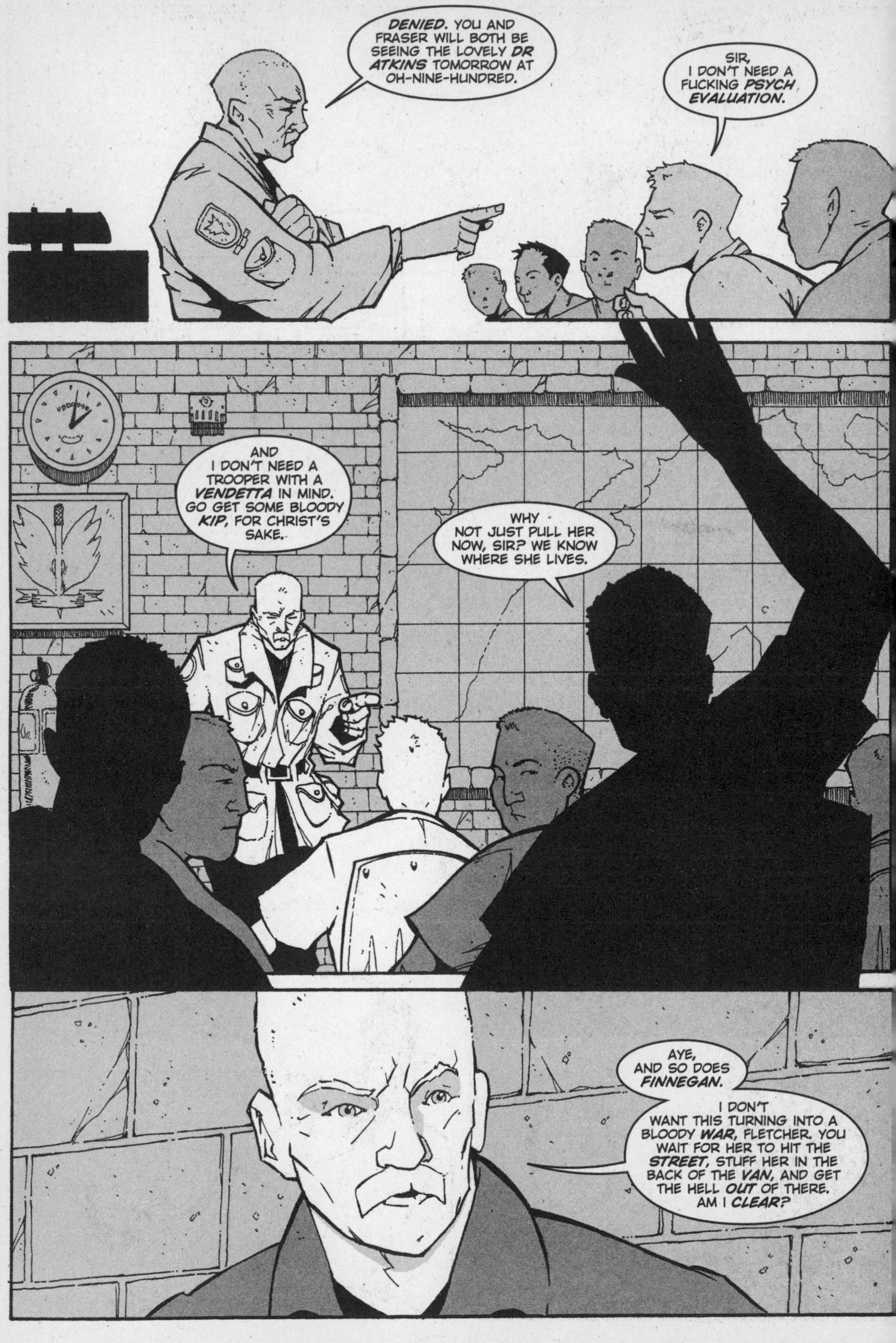
DENIED. YOU AND FRASER WILL BOTH BE SEEING THE LOVELY DR ATKINS TOMORROW AT OH-NINE-HUNDRED.
SIR, I DON'T NEED A FUCKING PSYCH EVALUATION.
AND I DON'T NEED A TROOPER WITH A VENDETTA IN MIND. GO GET SOME BLOODY KIP, FOR CHRIST'S SAKE.
WHY NOT JUST PULL HER NOW, SIR? WE KNOW WHERE SHE LIVES.
AYE, AND SO DOES FINNEGAN.
I DON'T WANT THIS TURNING INTO A BLOODY WAR, FLETCHER. YOU WAIT FOR HER TO HIT THE STREET, STUFF HER IN THE BACK OF THE VAN, AND GET THE HELL OUT OF THERE. AM I CLEAR?

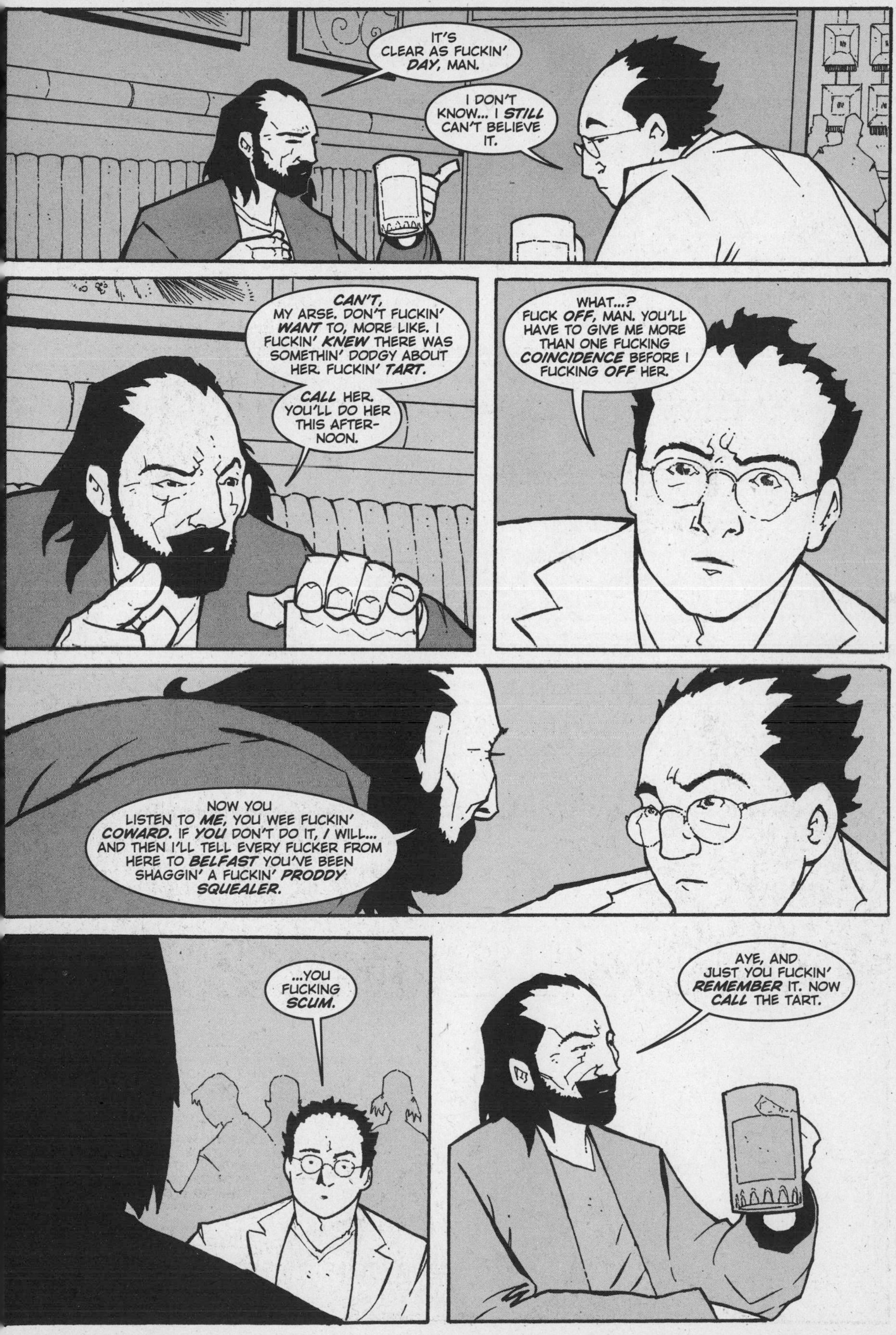
IT'S CLEAR AS FUCKIN' DAY, MAN.
I DON'T KNOW... I STILL CAN'T BELIEVE IT.
CAN'T, MY ARSE. DON'T FUCKIN' WANT TO, MORE LIKE. I FUCKIN' KNEW THERE WAS SOMETHIN' DODGY ABOUT HER. FUCKIN' TART.
CALL HER. YOU'LL DO HER THIS AFTER-NOON.
WHAT...? FUCK OFF, MAN. YOU'LL HAVE TO GIVE ME MORE THAN ONE FUCKING COINCIDENCE BEFORE I FUCKING OFF HER.
NOW YOU LISTEN TO ME, YOU WEE FUCKIN' COWARD. IF YOU DON'T DO IT, I WILL... AND THEN I'LL TELL EVERY FUCKER FROM HERE TO BELFAST YOU'VE BEEN SHAGGIN' A FUCKIN' PRODDY SQUEALER.
...YOU FUCKING SCUM.
AYE, AND JUST YOU FUCKIN' REMEMBER IT. NOW CALL THE TART.

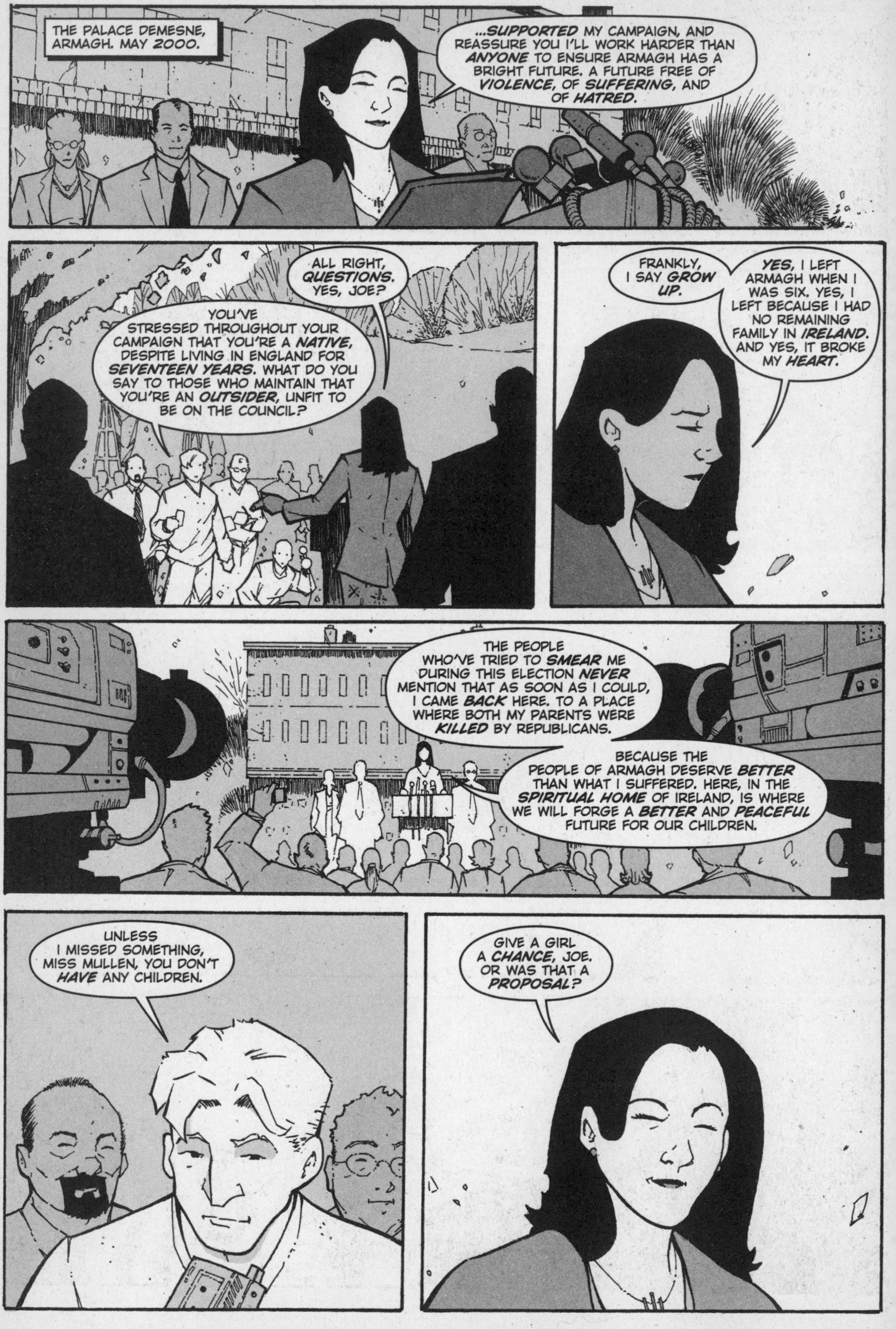
THE PALACE DEMESNE, ARMAGH. MAY 2000.
...SUPPORTED MY CAMPAIGN, AND REASSURE YOU I'LL WORK HARDER THAN ANYONE TO ENSURE ARMAGH HAS A BRIGHT FUTURE. A FUTURE FREE OF VIOLENCE, OF SUFFERING, AND OF HATRED.
ALL RIGHT, QUESTIONS. YES, JOE?
YOU'VE STRESSED THROUGHOUT YOUR CAMPAIGN THAT YOU'RE A NATIVE, DESPITE LIVING IN ENGLAND FOR SEVENTEEN YEARS. WHAT DO YOU SAY TO THOSE WHO MAINTAIN THAT YOU'RE AN OUTSIDER, UNFIT TO BE ON THE COUNCIL?
FRANKLY, I SAY GROW UP.
YES, I LEFT ARMAGH WHEN I WAS SIX. YES, I LEFT BECAUSE I HAD NO REMAINING FAMILY IN IRELAND. AND YES, IT BROKE MY HEART.
THE PEOPLE WHO'VE TRIED TO SMEAR ME DURING THIS ELECTION NEVER MENTION THAT AS SOON AS I COULD, I CAME BACK HERE. TO A PLACE WHERE BOTH MY PARENTS WERE KILLED BY REPUBLICANS.
BECAUSE THE PEOPLE OF ARMAGH DESERVE BETTER THAN WHAT I SUFFERED. HERE, IN THE SPIRITUAL HOME OF IRELAND, IS WHERE WE WILL FORGE A BETTER AND PEACEFUL FUTURE FOR OUR CHILDREN.
UNLESS I MISSED SOMETHING, MISS MULLEN, YOU DON'T HAVE ANY CHILDREN.
GIVE A GIRL A CHANCE, JOE. OR WAS THAT A PROPOSAL?

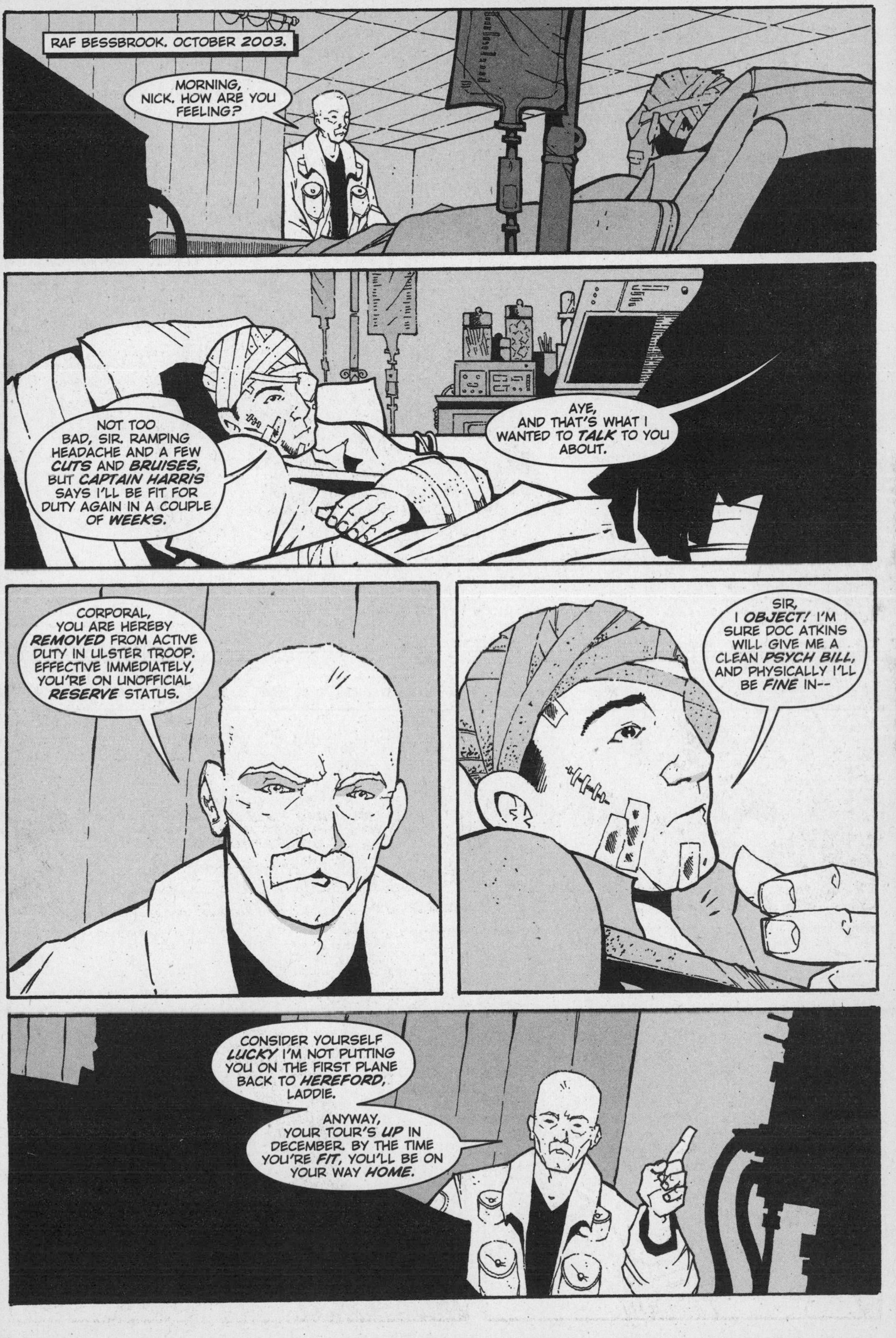
RAF BESSBROOK. OCTOBER 2003.
MORNING, NICK. HOW ARE YOU FEELING?
NOT TOO BAD, SIR. RAMPING HEADACHE AND A FEW CUTS AND BRUISES, BUT CAPTAIN HARRIS SAYS I'LL BE FIT FOR DUTY AGAIN IN A COUPLE OF WEEKS.
AYE, AND THAT'S WHAT I WANTED TO TALK TO YOU ABOUT.
CORPORAL, YOU ARE HEREBY REMOVED FROM ACTIVE DUTY IN ULSTER TROOP. EFFECTIVE IMMEDIATELY, YOU'RE ON UNOFFICIAL RESERVE STATUS.
SIR, I OBJECT! I'M SURE DOC ATKINS WILL GIVE ME A CLEAN PSYCH BILL, AND PHYSICALLY I'LL BE FINE IN--
CONSIDER YOURSELF LUCKY I'M NOT PUTTING YOU ON THE FIRST PLANE BACK TO HEREFORD, LADDIE.
ANYWAY, YOUR TOUR'S UP IN DECEMBER. BY THE TIME YOU'RE FIT, YOU'LL BE ON YOUR WAY HOME.

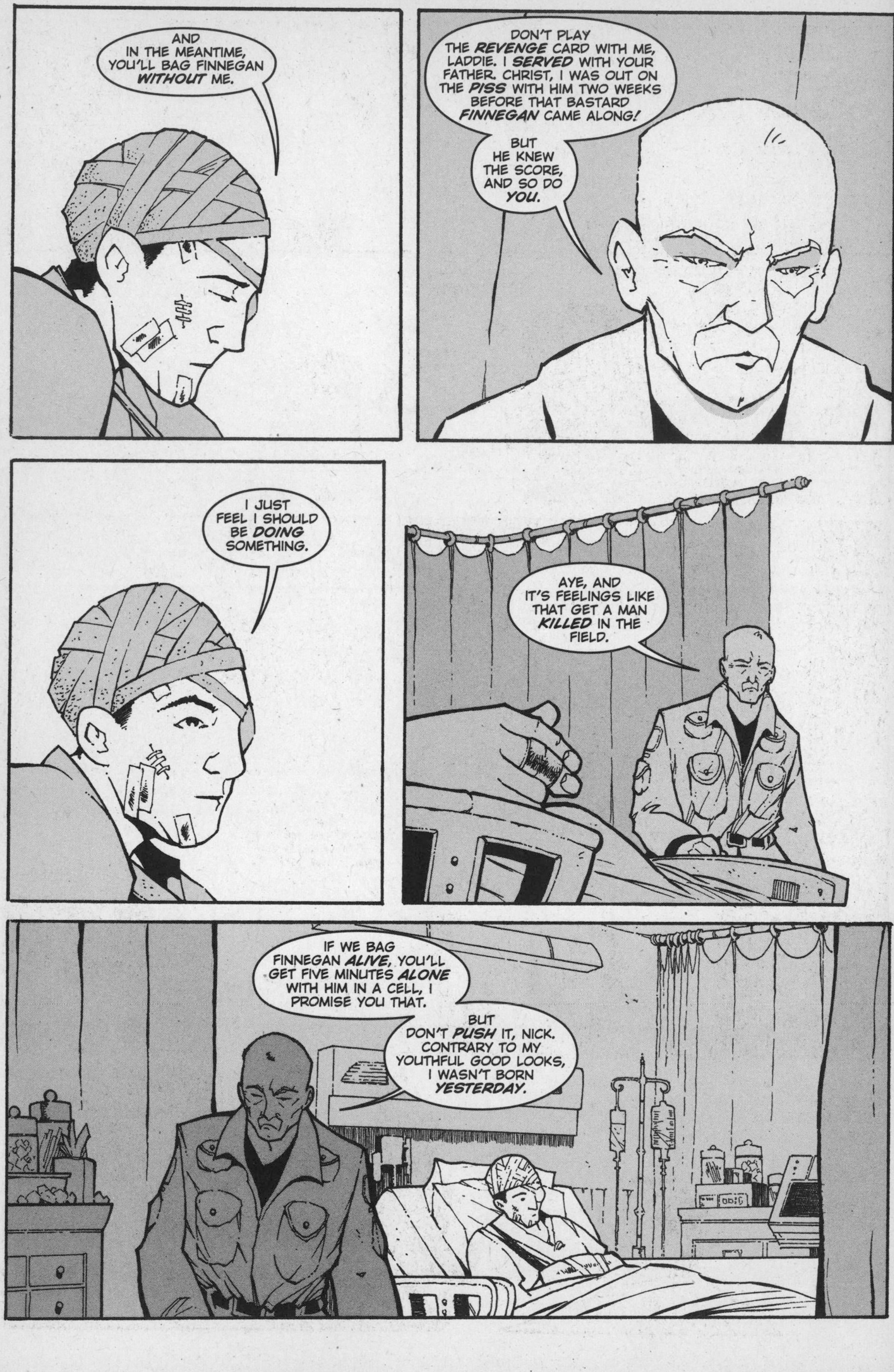
AND IN THE MEANTIME, YOU'LL BAG FINNEGAN WITHOUT ME.
DON'T PLAY THE REVENGE CARD WITH ME, LADDIE. I SERVED WITH YOUR FATHER. CHRIST, I WAS OUT ON THE PISS WITH HIM TWO WEEKS BEFORE THAT BASTARD FINNEGAN CAME ALONG!
BUT HE KNEW THE SCORE, AND SO DO YOU.
I JUST FEEL I SHOULD BE DOING SOMETHING.
AYE, AND IT'S FEELINGS LIKE THAT GET A MAN KILLED IN THE FIELD.
IF WE BAG FINNEGAN ALIVE, YOU'LL GET FIVE MINUTES ALONE WITH HIM IN A CELL, I PROMISE YOU THAT.
BUT DON'T PUSH IT, NICK. CONTRARY TO MY YOUTHFUL GOOD LOOKS, I WASN'T BORN YESTERDAY.

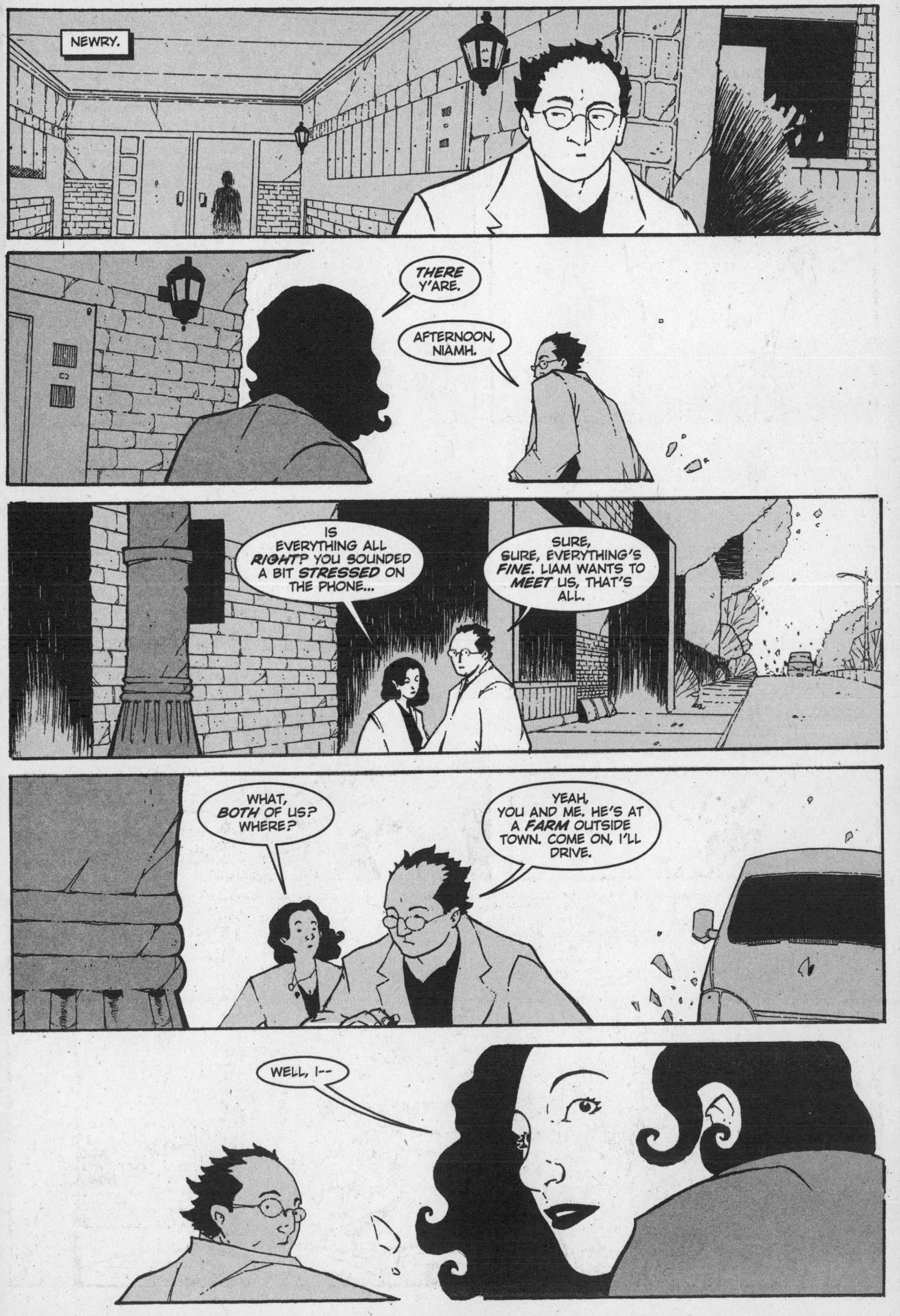
NEWRY.
THERE Y'ARE.
AFTERNOON, NIAMH.
IS EVERYTHING ALL RIGHT? YOU SOUNDED A BIT STRESSED ON THE PHONE...
SURE, SURE, EVERYTHING'S FINE. LIAM WANTS TO MEET US, THAT'S ALL.
WHAT, BOTH OF US? WHERE?
YEAH, YOU AND ME. HE'S AT A FARM OUTSIDE TOWN. COME ON, I'LL DRIVE.
WELL, I--

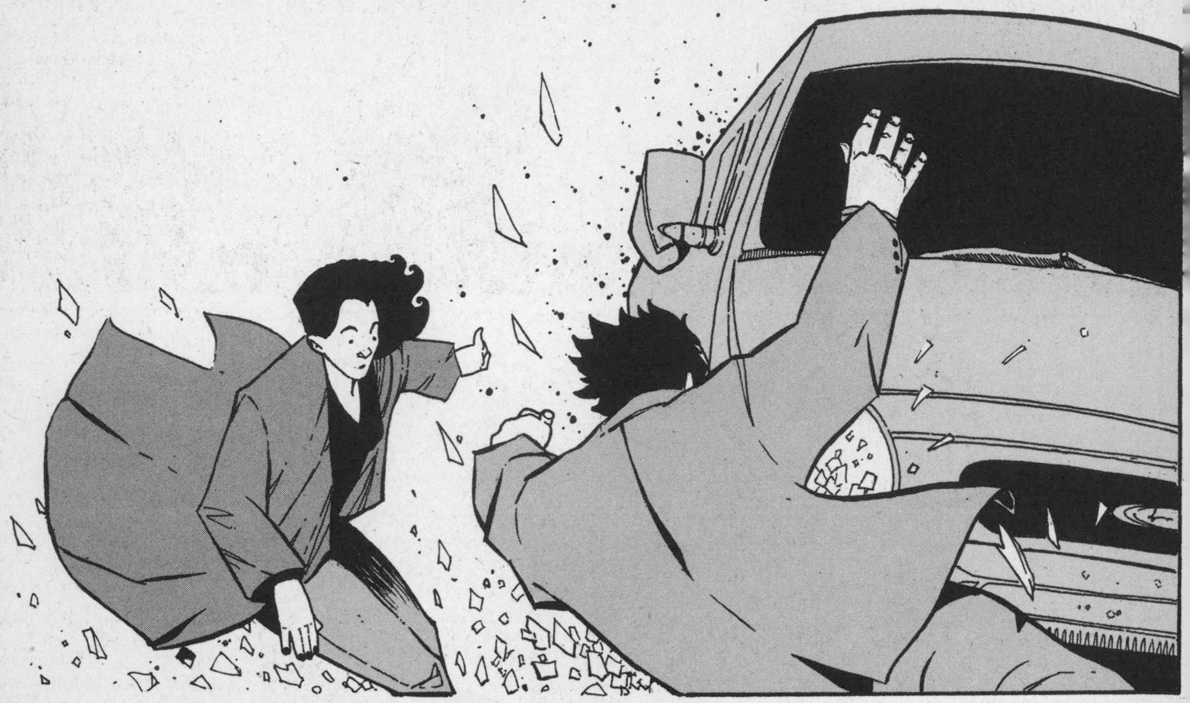

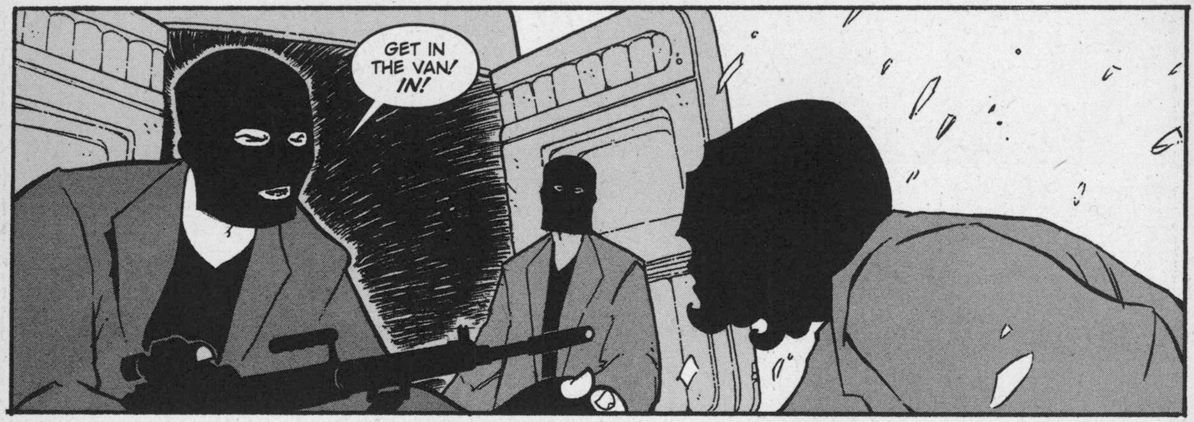
GET IN THE VAN! IN!

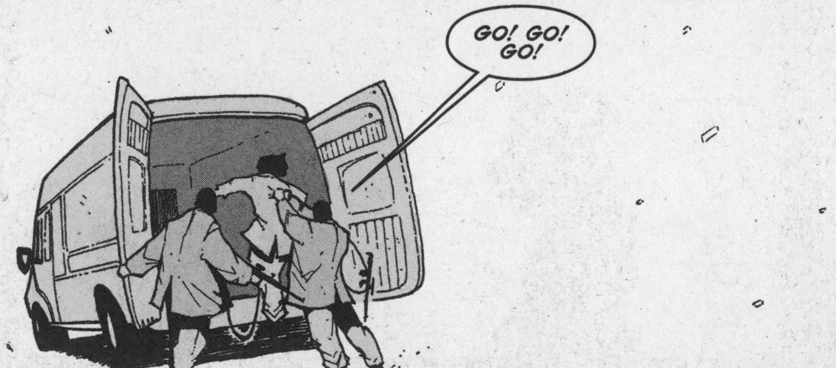
GO! GO! GO!

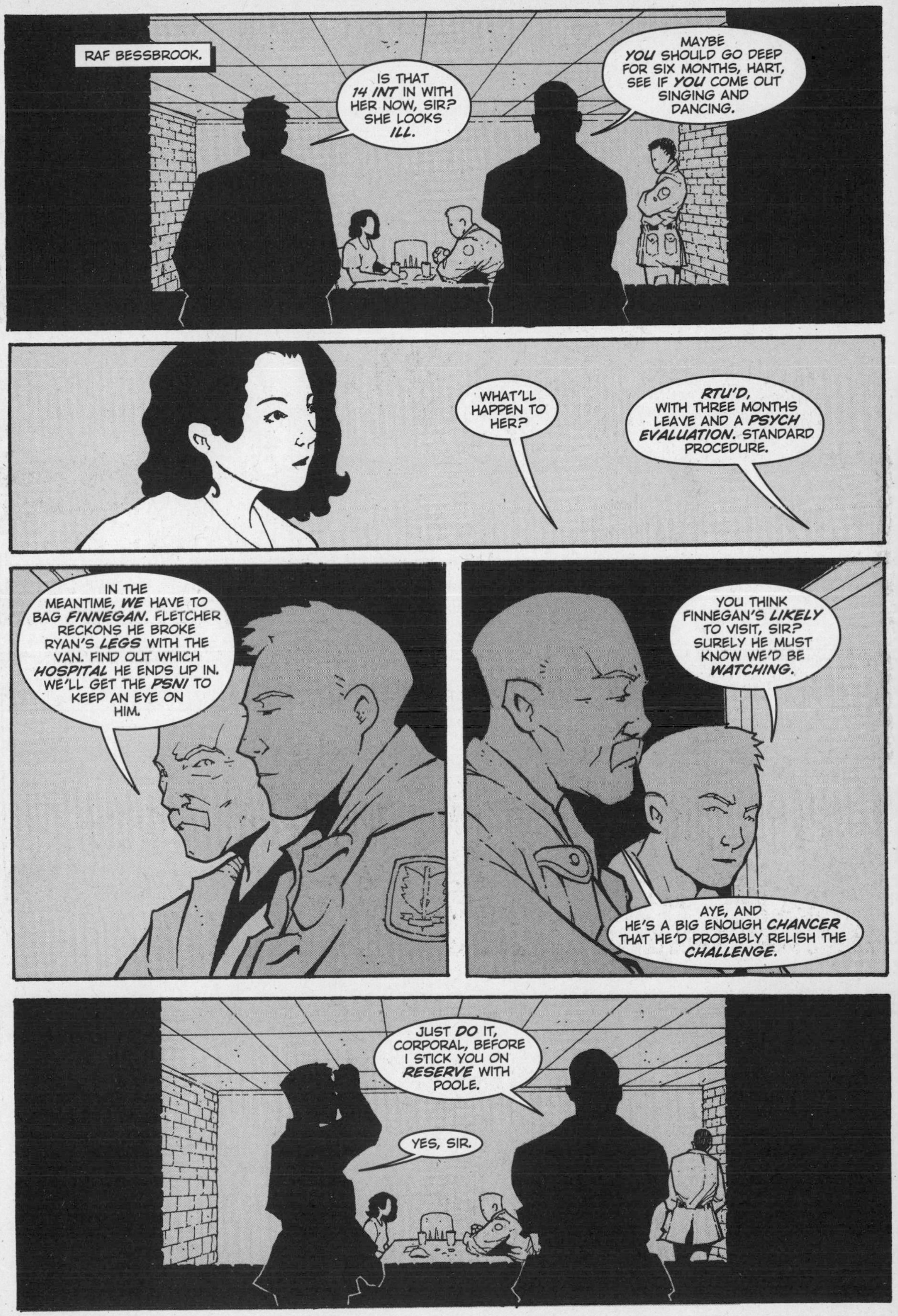
RAF BESSBROOK.
IS THAT 14 INT IN WITH HER NOW, SIR? SHE LOOKS ILL.
MAYBE YOU SHOULD GO DEEP FOR SIX MONTHS, HART, SEE IF YOU COME OUT SINGING AND DANCING.
WHAT'LL HAPPEN TO HER?
RTU'D, WITH THREE MONTHS LEAVE AND A PSYCH EVALUATION. STANDARD PROCEDURE.
IN THE MEANTIME, WE HAVE TO BAG FINNEGAN. FLETCHER RECKONS HE BROKE RYAN'S LEGS WITH THE VAN. FIND OUT WHICH HOSPITAL HE ENDS UP IN. WE'LL GET THE PSNI TO KEEP AN EYE ON HIM.
YOU THINK FINNEGAN'S LIKELY TO VISIT, SIR? SURELY HE MUST KNOW WE'D BE WATCHING.
AYE, AND HE'S A BIG ENOUGH CHANCER THAT HE'D PROBABLY RELISH THE CHALLENGE.
JUST DO IT, CORPORAL, BEFORE I STICK YOU ON RESERVE WITH POOLE.
YES, SIR.

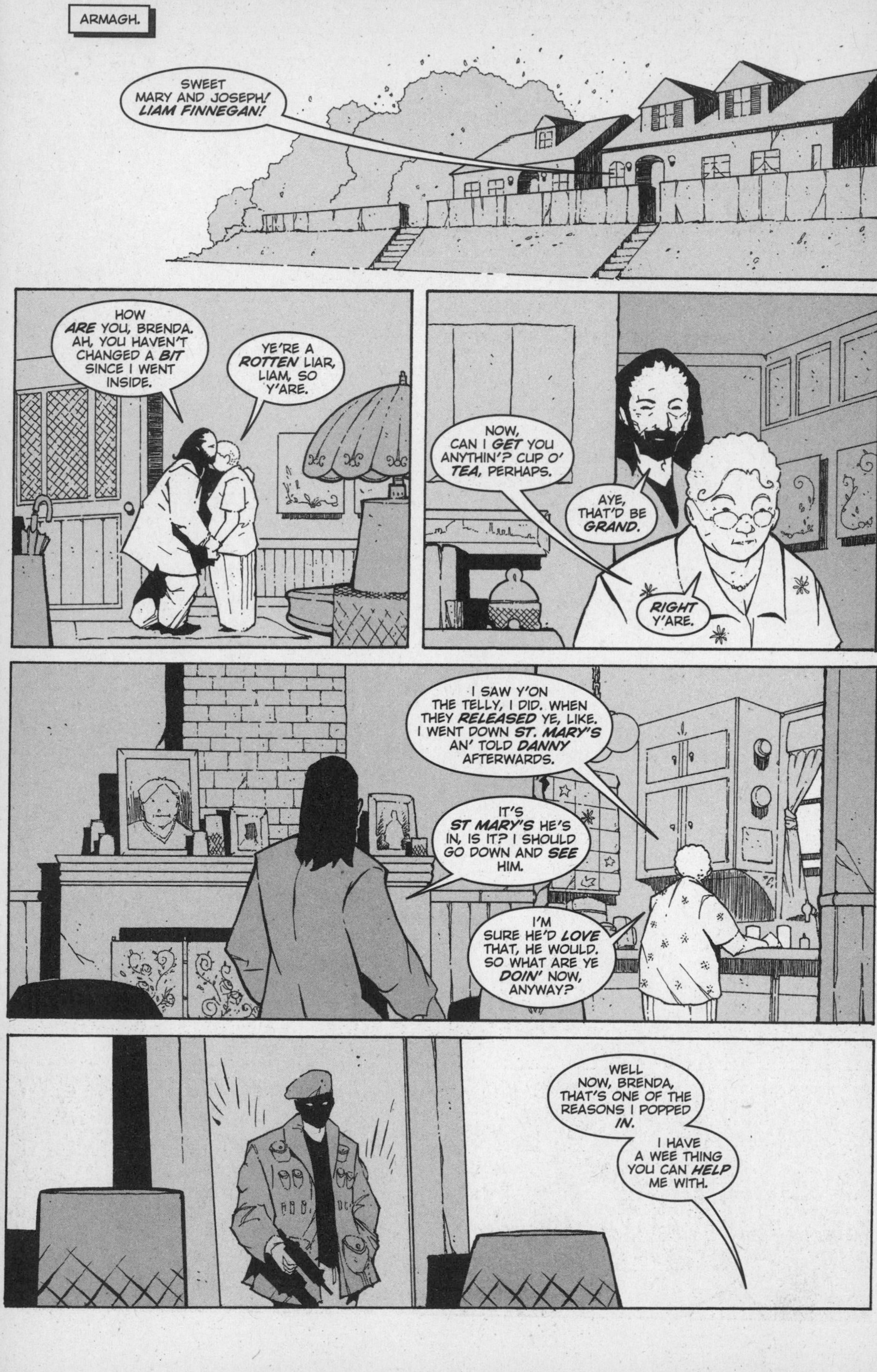
ARMAGH.
SWEET MARY AND JOSEPH! LIAM FINNEGAN!
HOW ARE YOU, BRENDA. AH, YOU HAVEN'T CHANGED A BIT SINCE I WENT INSIDE.
YE'RE A ROTTEN LIAR, LIAM, SO Y'ARE.
NOW, CAN I GET YOU ANYTHIN'? CUP O' TEA, PERHAPS.
AYE, THAT'D BE GRAND.
RIGHT Y'ARE.
I SAW Y'ON THE TELLY, I DID. WHEN THEY RELEASED YE, LIKE. I WENT DOWN ST. MARY'S AN' TOLD DANNY AFTERWARDS.
IT'S ST MARY'S HE'S IN, IS IT? I SHOULD GO DOWN AND SEE HIM.
I'M SURE HE'D LOVE THAT, HE WOULD. SO WHAT ARE YE DOIN' NOW, ANYWAY?
WELL NOW, BRENDA, THAT'S ONE OF THE REASONS I POPPED IN.
I HAVE A WEE THING YOU CAN HELP ME WITH.

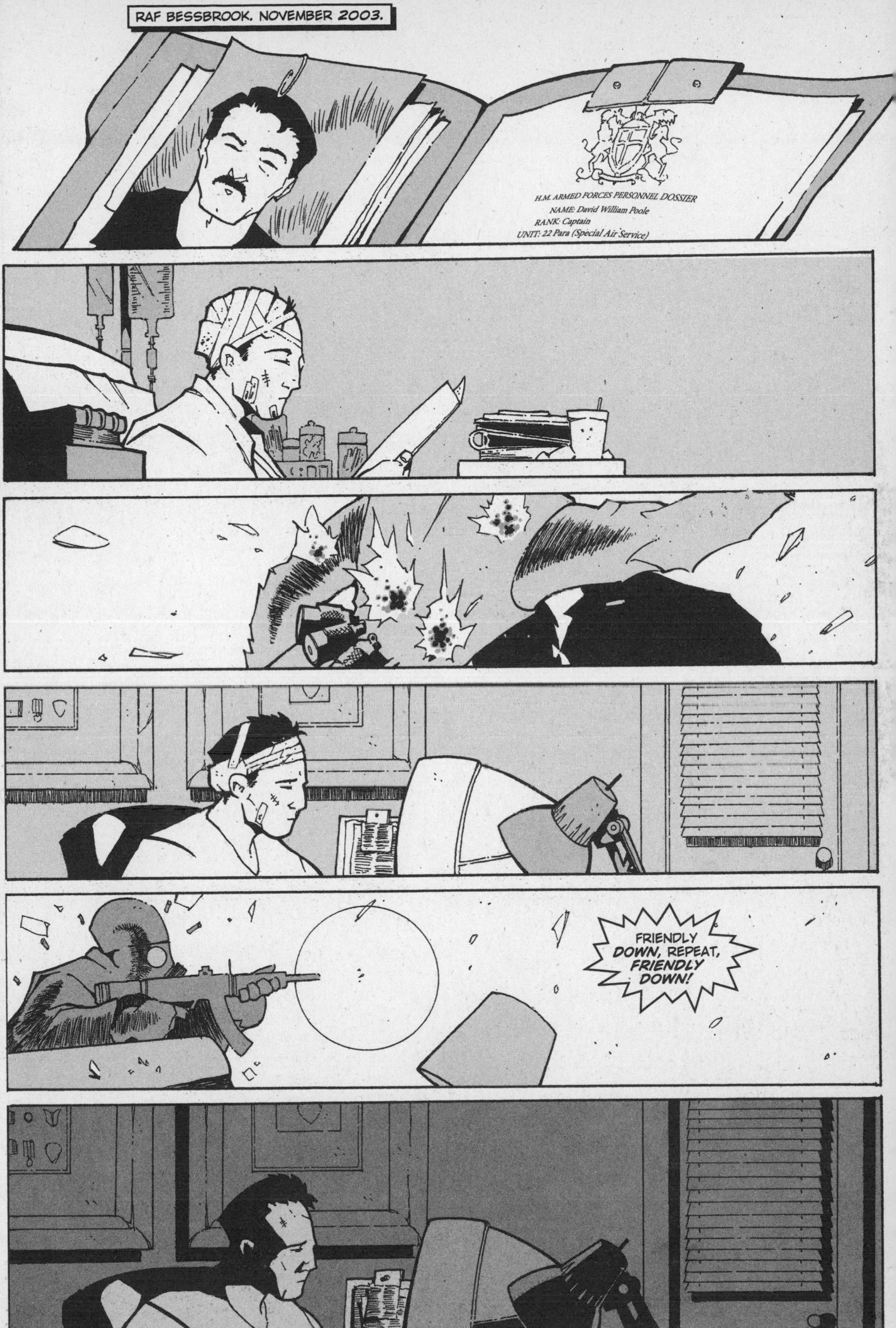
RAF BESSBROOK. NOVEMBER 2003.
H.M. ARMED FORCES PERSONNEL DOSSIER
NAME: David William Poole
RANK: Captain
UNIT: 22 Para (Special Air Service)
FRIENDLY DOWN, REPEAT, FRIENDLY DOWN!

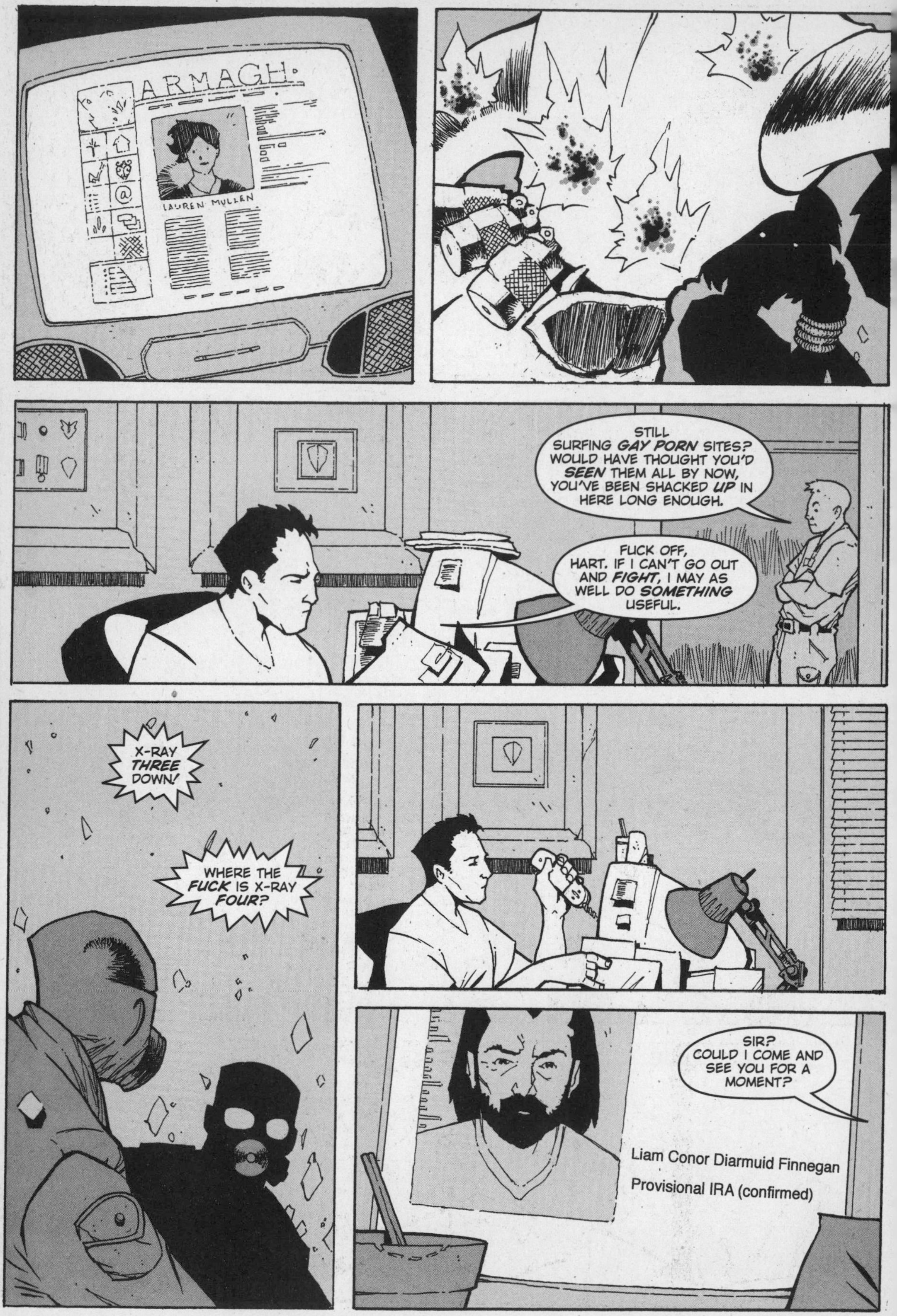
ARMAGH
LAUREN MULLEN
STILL SURFING GAY PORN SITES? WOULD HAVE THOUGHT YOU'D SEEN THEM ALL BY NOW, YOU'VE BEEN SHACKED UP IN HERE LONG ENOUGH.
FUCK OFF, HART. IF I CAN'T GO OUT AND FIGHT, I MAY AS WELL DO SOMETHING USEFUL.
X-RAY THREE DOWN!
WHERE THE FUCK IS X-RAY FOUR?
SIR? COULD I COME AND SEE YOU FOR A MOMENT?
Liam Conor Diarmuid Finnegan
Provisional IRA (confirmed)

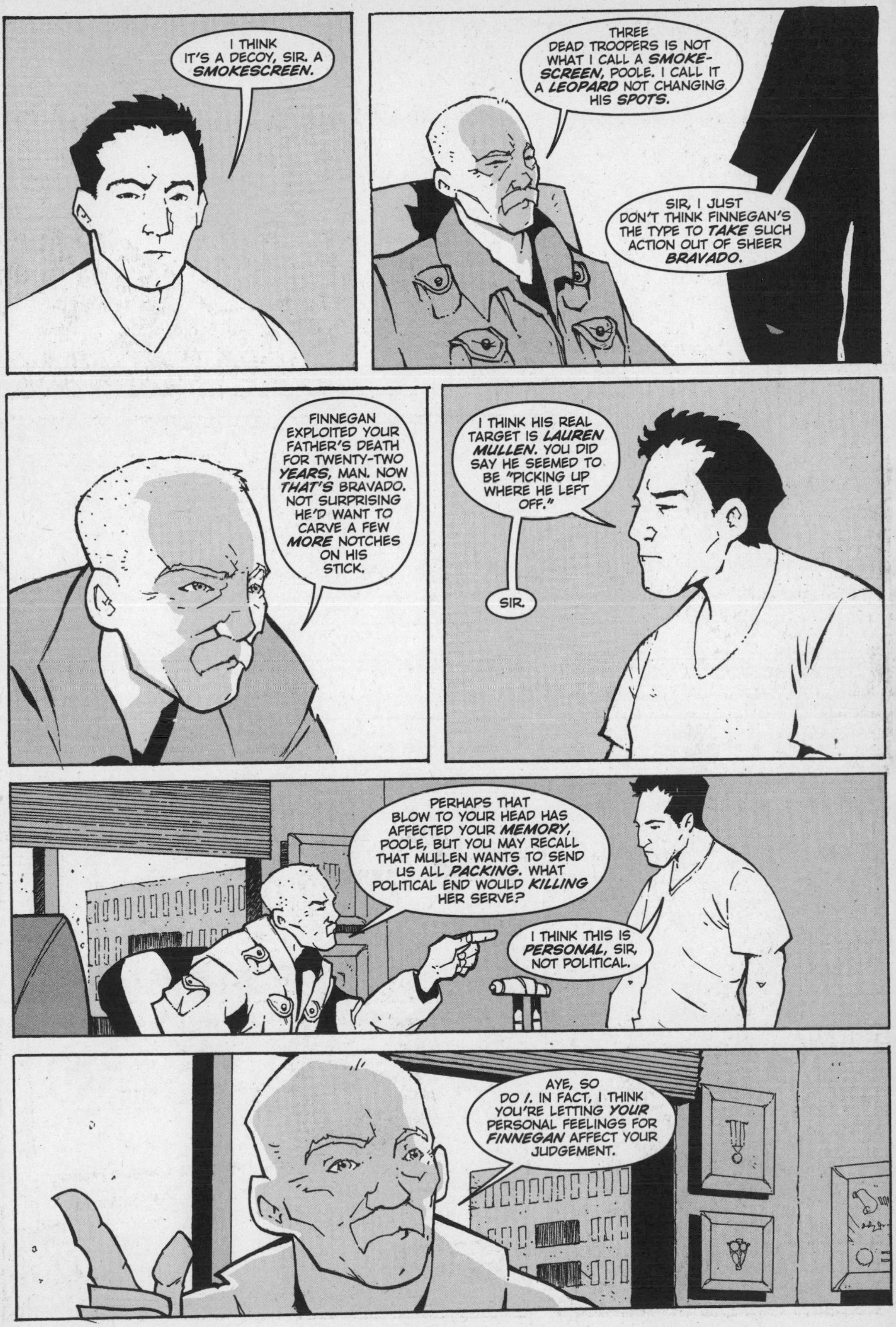
I THINK IT'S A DECOY, SIR. A SMOKESCREEN.
THREE DEAD TROOPERS IS NOT WHAT I CALL A SMOKE-SCREEN, POOLE. I CALL IT A LEOPARD NOT CHANGING HIS SPOTS.
SIR, I JUST DON'T THINK FINNEGAN'S THE TYPE TO TAKE SUCH ACTION OUT OF SHEER BRAVADO.
FINNEGAN EXPLOITED YOUR FATHER'S DEATH FOR TWENTY-TWO YEARS, MAN. NOW THAT'S BRAVADO. NOT SURPRISING HE'D WANT TO CARVE A FEW MORE NOTCHES ON HIS STICK.
I THINK HIS REAL TARGET IS LAUREN MULLEN. YOU DID SAY HE SEEMED TO BE "PICKING UP WHERE HE LEFT OFF."
SIR.
PERHAPS THAT BLOW TO YOUR HEAD HAS AFFECTED YOUR MEMORY, POOLE, BUT YOU MAY RECALL THAT MULLEN WANTS TO SEND US ALL PACKING. WHAT POLITICAL END WOULD KILLING HER SERVE?
I THINK THIS IS PERSONAL, SIR, NOT POLITICAL.
AYE, SO DO I. IN FACT, I THINK YOU'RE LETTING YOUR PERSONAL FEELINGS FOR FINNEGAN AFFECT YOUR JUDGEMENT.

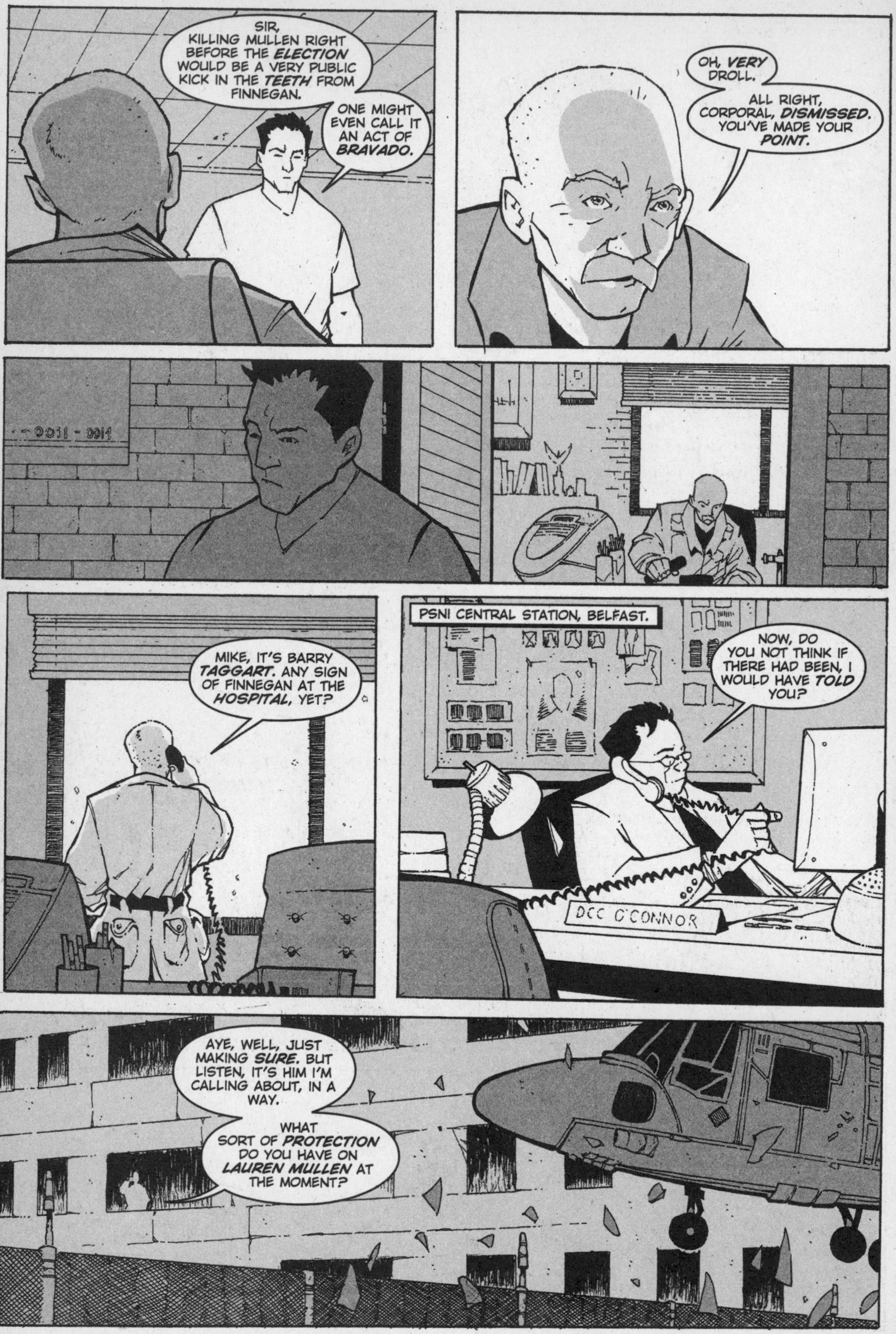
SIR, KILLING MULLEN RIGHT BEFORE THE ELECTION WOULD BE A VERY PUBLIC KICK IN THE TEETH FROM FINNEGAN.
ONE MIGHT EVEN CALL IT AN ACT OF BRAVADO.
OH, VERY DROLL.
ALL RIGHT, CORPORAL, DISMISSED. YOU'VE MADE YOUR POINT.
MIKE, IT'S BARRY TAGGART. ANY SIGN OF FINNEGAN AT THE HOSPITAL, YET?
PSNI CENTRAL STATION, BELFAST.
NOW, DO YOU NOT THINK IF THERE HAD BEEN, I WOULD HAVE TOLD YOU?
DCC O'CONNOR
AYE, WELL, JUST MAKING SURE. BUT LISTEN, IT'S HIM I'M CALLING ABOUT, IN A WAY.
WHAT SORT OF PROTECTION DO YOU HAVE ON LAUREN MULLEN AT THE MOMENT?

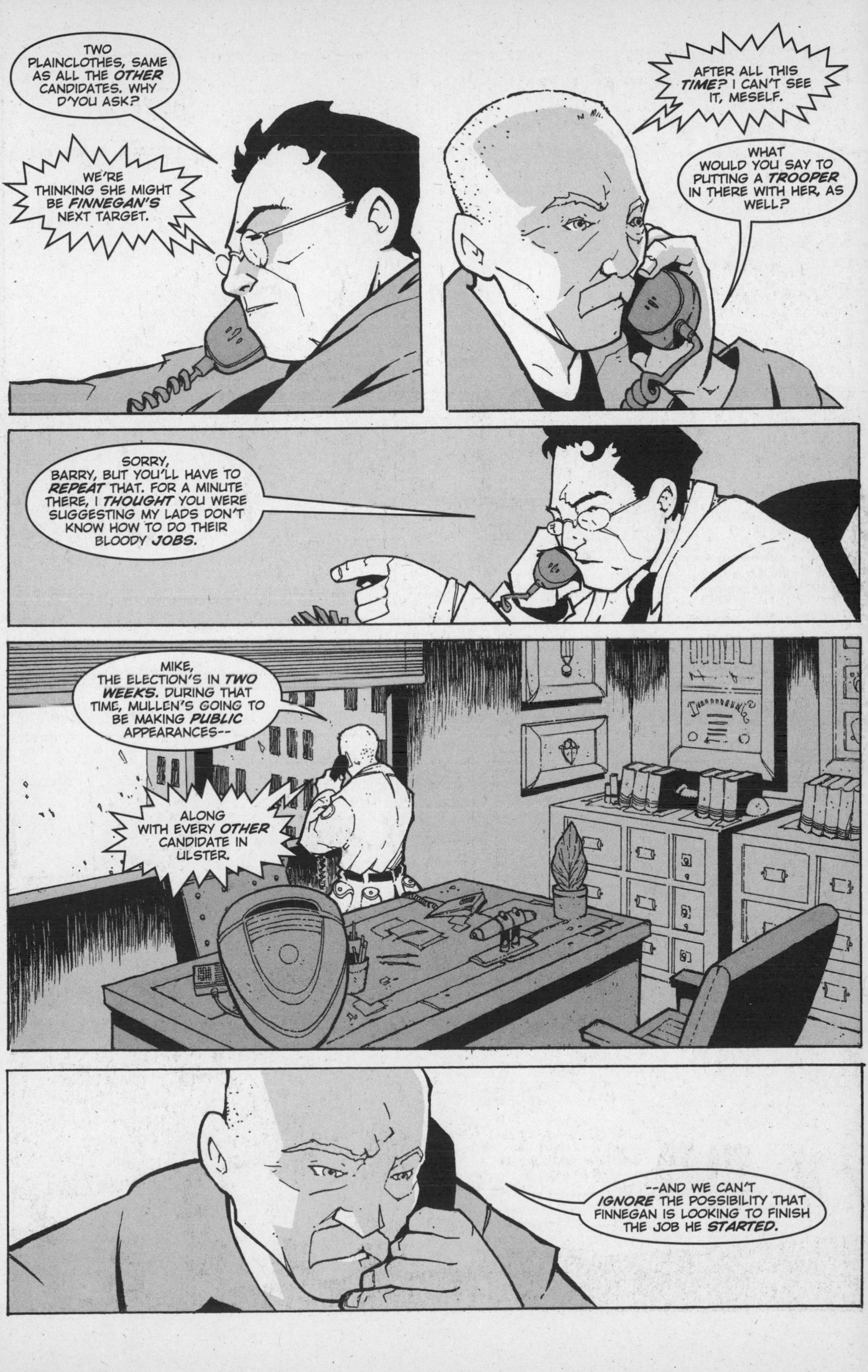
TWO PLAINCLOTHES, SAME AS ALL THE OTHER CANDIDATES. WHY D'YOU ASK?
WE'RE THINKING SHE MIGHT BE FINNEGAN'S NEXT TARGET.
AFTER ALL THIS TIME? I CAN'T SEE IT, MESELF.
WHAT WOULD YOU SAY TO PUTTING A TROOPER IN THERE WITH HER, AS WELL?
SORRY, BARRY, BUT YOU'LL HAVE TO REPEAT THAT. FOR A MINUTE THERE, I THOUGHT YOU WERE SUGGESTING MY LADS DON'T KNOW HOW TO DO THEIR BLOODY JOBS.
MIKE, THE ELECTION'S IN TWO WEEKS. DURING THAT TIME, MULLEN'S GOING TO BE MAKING PUBLIC APPEARANCES--
ALONG WITH EVERY OTHER CANDIDATE IN ULSTER.
--AND WE CAN'T IGNORE THE POSSIBILITY THAT FINNEGAN IS LOOKING TO FINISH THE JOB HE STARTED.

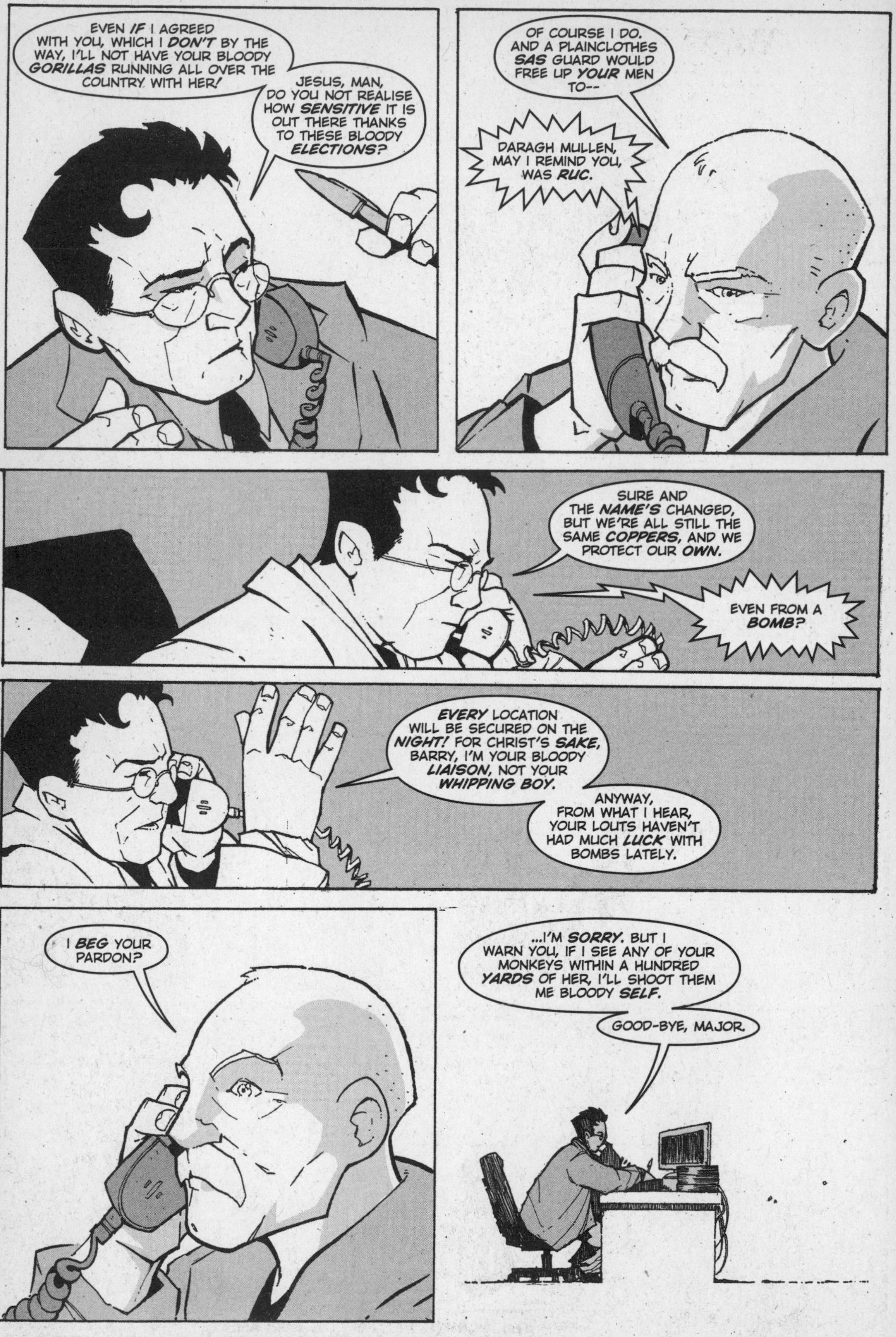
EVEN IF I AGREED WITH YOU, WHICH I DON'T BY THE WAY, I'LL NOT HAVE YOUR BLOODY GORILLAS RUNNING ALL OVER THE COUNTRY WITH HER!
JESUS, MAN, DO YOU NOT REALISE HOW SENSITIVE IT IS OUT THERE THANKS TO THESE BLOODY ELECTIONS?
OF COURSE I DO. AND A PLAINCLOTHES SAS GUARD WOULD FREE UP YOUR MEN TO--
DARAGH MULLEN, MAY I REMIND YOU, WAS RUC.
SURE AND THE NAME'S CHANGED, BUT WE'RE ALL STILL THE SAME COPPERS, AND WE PROTECT OUR OWN.
EVEN FROM A BOMB?
EVERY LOCATION WILL BE SECURED ON THE NIGHT! FOR CHRIST'S SAKE, BARRY, I'M YOUR BLOODY LIAISON, NOT YOUR WHIPPING BOY.
ANYWAY, FROM WHAT I HEAR, YOUR LOUTS HAVEN'T HAD MUCH LUCK WITH BOMBS LATELY.
I BEG YOUR PARDON?
...I'M SORRY. BUT I WARN YOU, IF I SEE ANY OF YOUR MONKEYS WITHIN A HUNDRED YARDS OF HER, I'LL SHOOT THEM ME BLOODY SELF.
GOOD-BYE, MAJOR.

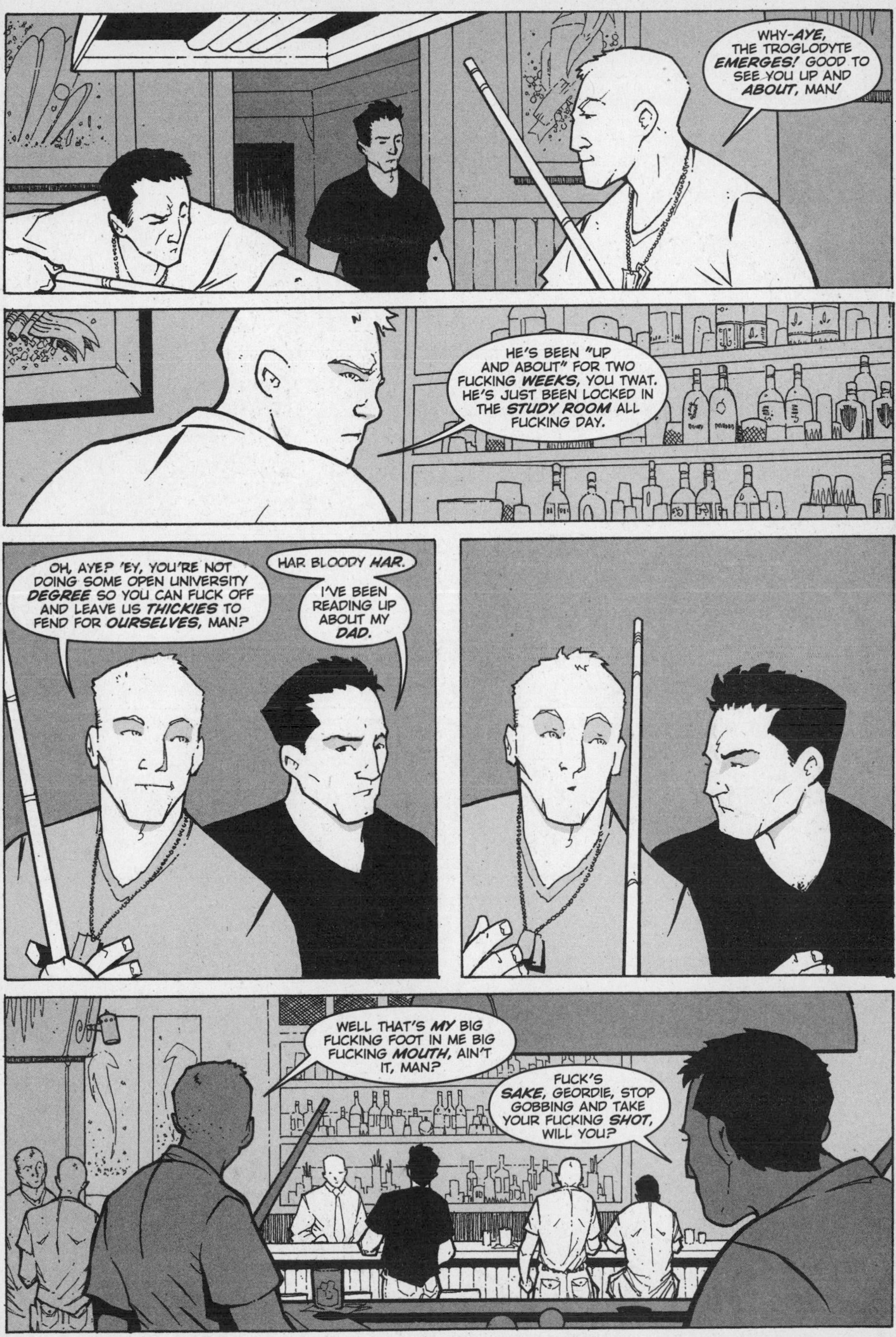
WHY-AYE, THE TROGLODYTE EMERGES! GOOD TO SEE YOU UP AND ABOUT, MAN!
HE'S BEEN "UP AND ABOUT" FOR TWO FUCKING WEEKS, YOU TWAT. HE'S JUST BEEN LOCKED IN THE STUDY ROOM ALL FUCKING DAY.
OH, AYE? 'EY, YOU'RE NOT DOING SOME OPEN UNIVERSITY DEGREE SO YOU CAN FUCK OFF AND LEAVE US THICKIES TO FEND FOR OURSELVES, MAN?
HAR BLOODY HAR.
I'VE BEEN READING UP ABOUT MY DAD.
WELL THAT'S MY BIG FUCKING FOOT IN ME BIG FUCKING MOUTH, AIN'T IT, MAN?
FUCK'S SAKE, GEORDIE, STOP GOBBING AND TAKE YOUR FUCKING SHOT, WILL YOU?

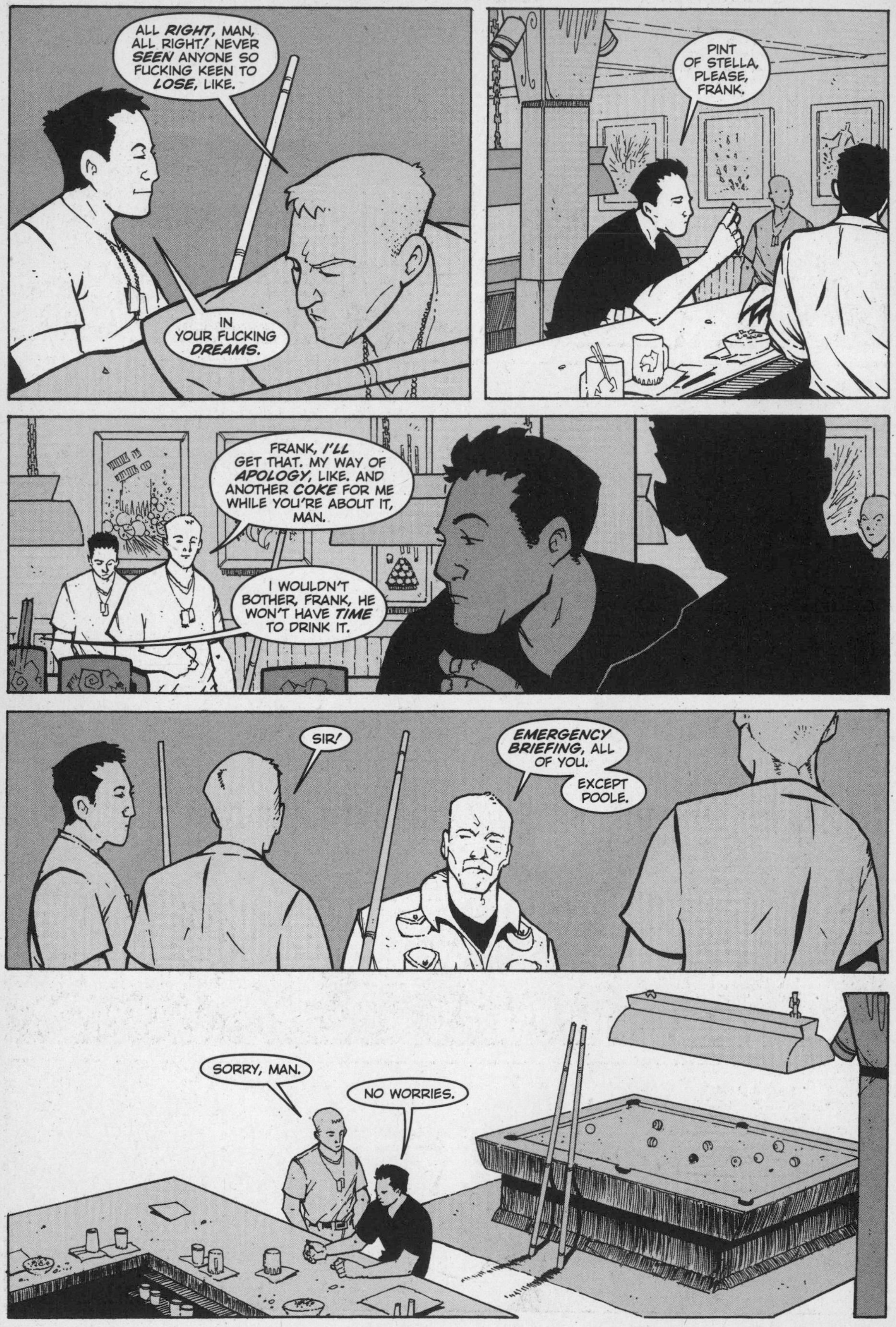
ALL RIGHT, MAN, ALL RIGHT! NEVER SEEN ANYONE SO FUCKING KEEN TO LOSE, LIKE.
IN YOUR FUCKING DREAMS.
PINT OF STELLA, PLEASE, FRANK.
FRANK, I'LL GET THAT. MY WAY OF APOLOGY, LIKE. AND ANOTHER COKE FOR ME WHILE YOU'RE ABOUT IT, MAN.
I WOULDN'T BOTHER, FRANK, HE WON'T HAVE TIME TO DRINK IT.
SIR!
EMERGENCY BRIEFING, ALL OF YOU.
EXCEPT POOLE.
SORRY, MAN.
NO WORRIES.

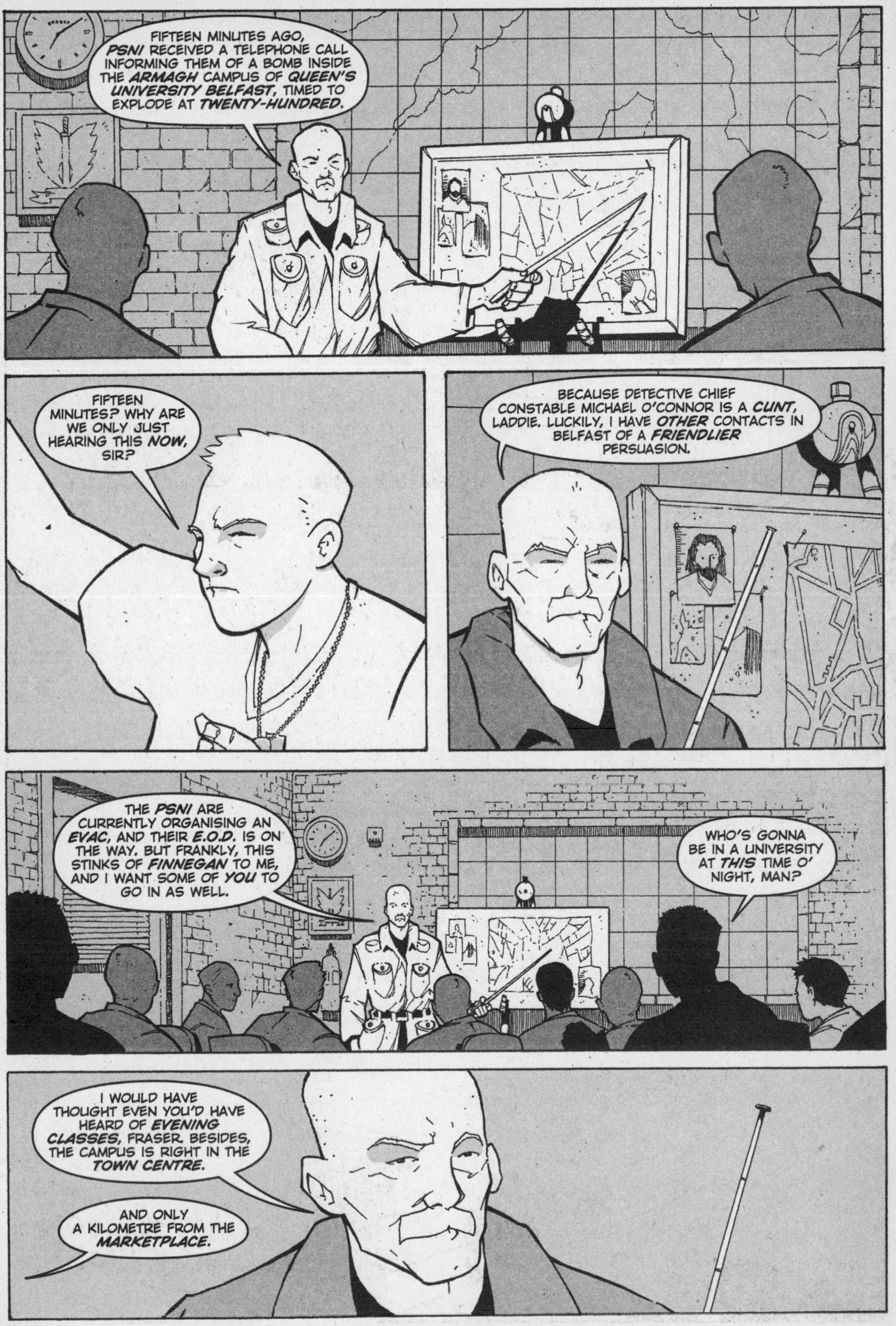
FIFTEEN MINUTES AGO, PSNI RECEIVED A TELEPHONE CALL INFORMING THEM OF A BOMB INSIDE THE ARMAGH CAMPUS OF QUEEN'S UNIVERSITY BELFAST, TIMED TO EXPLODE AT TWENTY-HUNDRED.
FIFTEEN MINUTES? WHY ARE WE ONLY JUST HEARING THIS NOW, SIR?
BECAUSE DETECTIVE CHIEF CONSTABLE MICHAEL O'CONNOR IS A CUNT, LADDIE. LUCKILY, I HAVE OTHER CONTACTS IN BELFAST OF A FRIENDLIER PERSUASION.
THE PSNI ARE CURRENTLY ORGANISING AN EVAC, AND THEIR E.O.D. IS ON THE WAY. BUT FRANKLY, THIS STINKS OF FINNEGAN TO ME, AND I WANT SOME OF YOU TO GO IN AS WELL.
WHO'S GONNA BE IN A UNIVERSITY AT THIS TIME O' NIGHT, MAN?
I WOULD HAVE THOUGHT EVEN YOU'D HAVE HEARD OF EVENING CLASSES, FRASER. BESIDES, THE CAMPUS IS RIGHT IN THE TOWN CENTRE.
AND ONLY A KILOMETRE FROM THE MARKETPLACE.

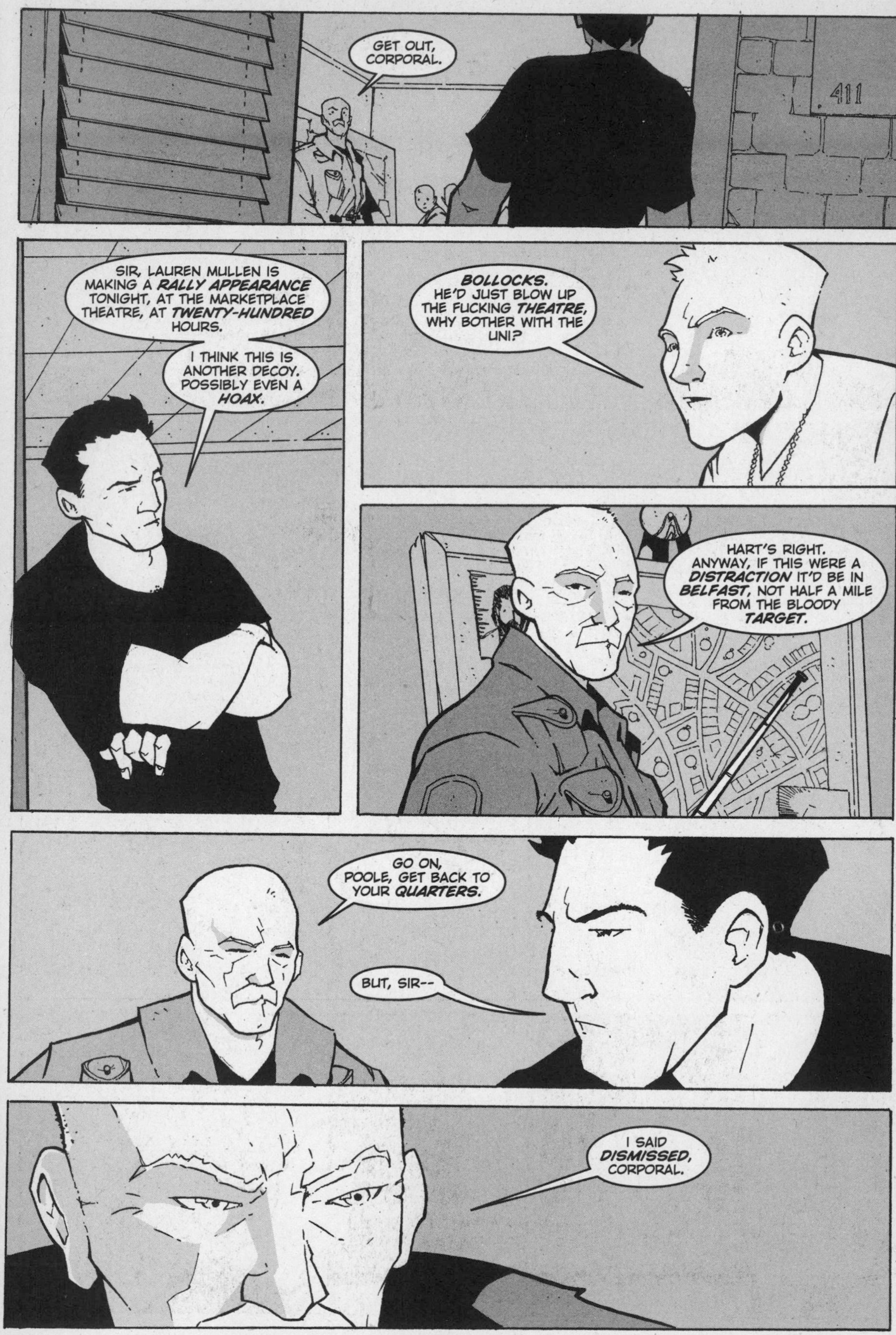
GET OUT, CORPORAL.
411
SIR, LAUREN MULLEN IS MAKING A RALLY APPEARANCE TONIGHT, AT THE MARKETPLACE THEATRE, AT TWENTY-HUNDRED HOURS.
I THINK THIS IS ANOTHER DECOY. POSSIBLY EVEN A HOAX.
BOLLOCKS. HE'D JUST BLOW UP THE FUCKING THEATRE, WHY BOTHER WITH THE UNI?
HART'S RIGHT. ANYWAY, IF THIS WERE A DISTRACTION IT'D BE IN BELFAST, NOT HALF A MILE FROM THE BLOODY TARGET.
GO ON, POOLE, GET BACK TO YOUR QUARTERS.
BUT, SIR--
I SAID DISMISSED, CORPORAL.

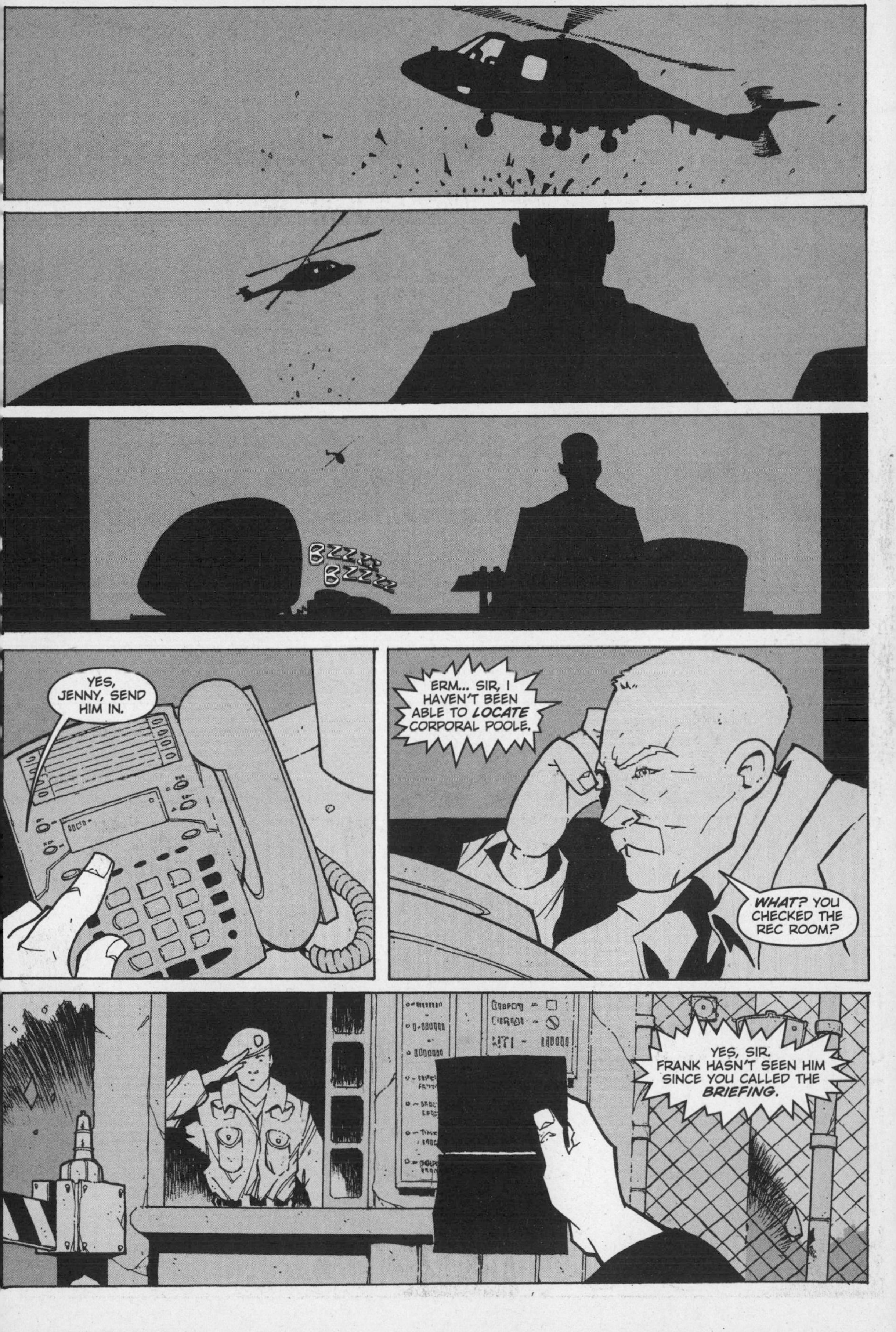
BZZZT BZZZZ
YES, JENNY, SEND HIM IN.
ERM... SIR, I HAVEN'T BEEN ABLE TO LOCATE CORPORAL POOLE.
WHAT? YOU CHECKED THE REC ROOM?
YES, SIR. FRANK HASN'T SEEN HIM SINCE YOU CALLED THE BRIEFING.

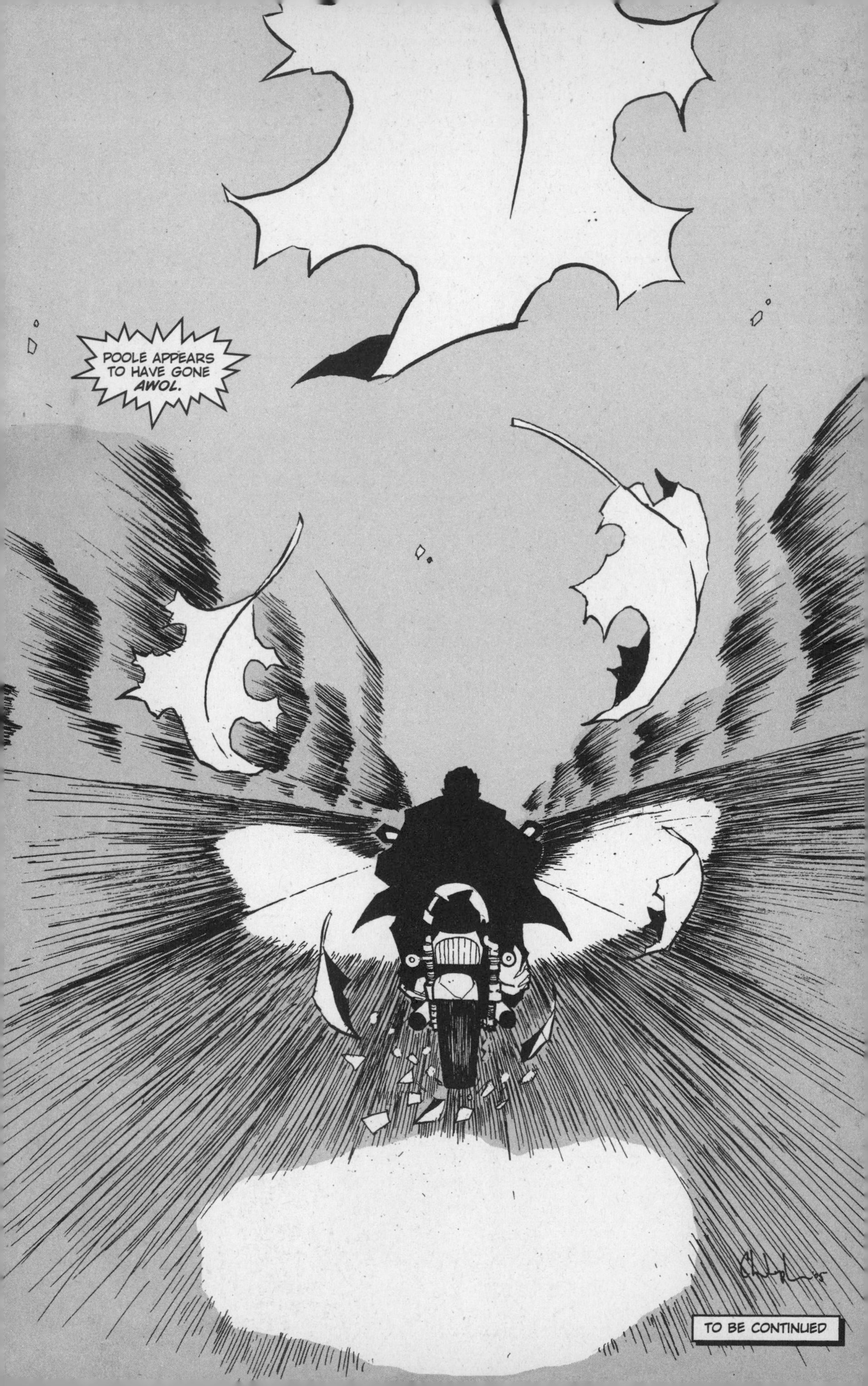
POOLE APPEARS TO HAVE GONE AWOL.
TO BE CONTINUED

CHAPTER 3

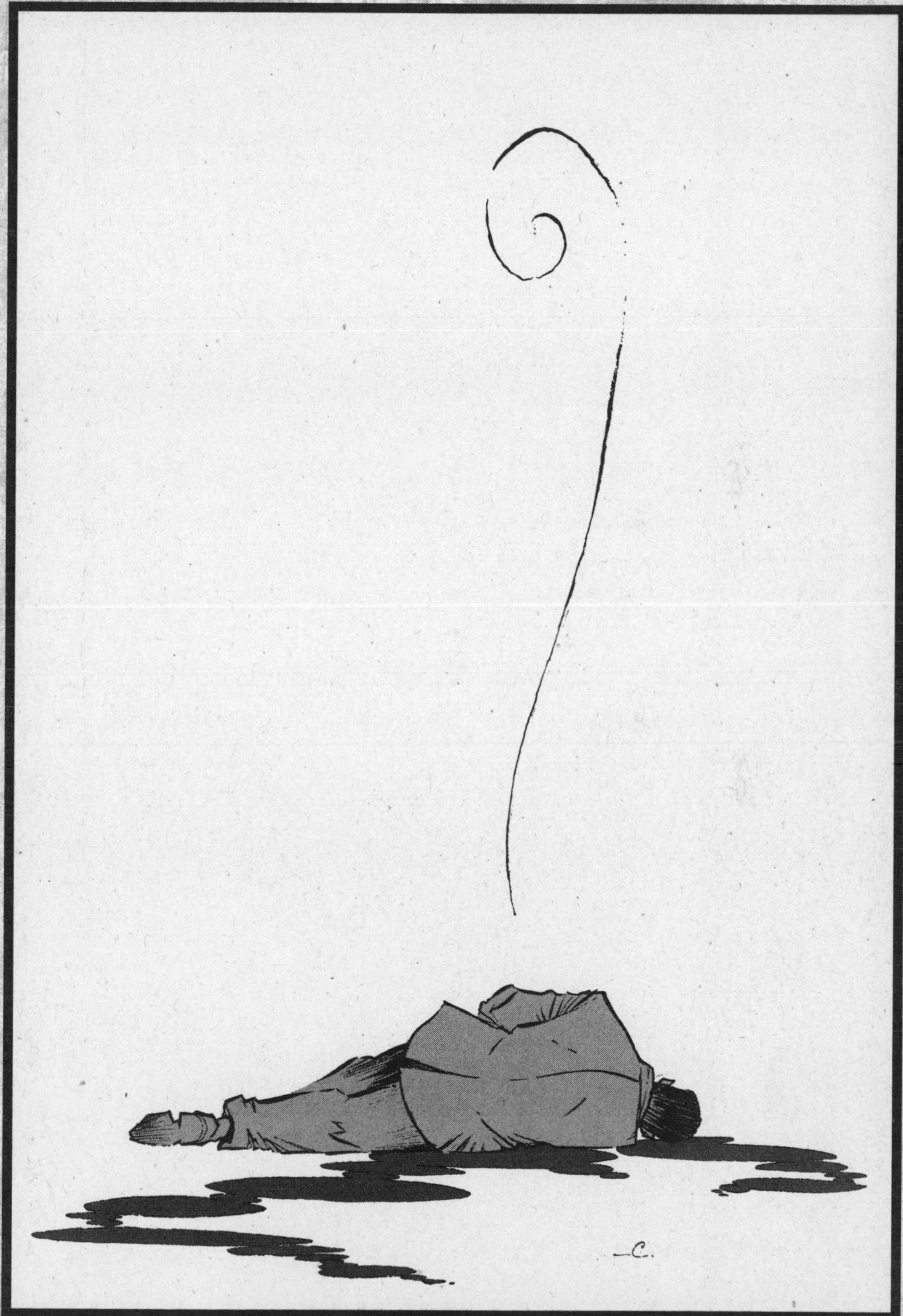
—C.

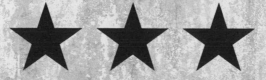

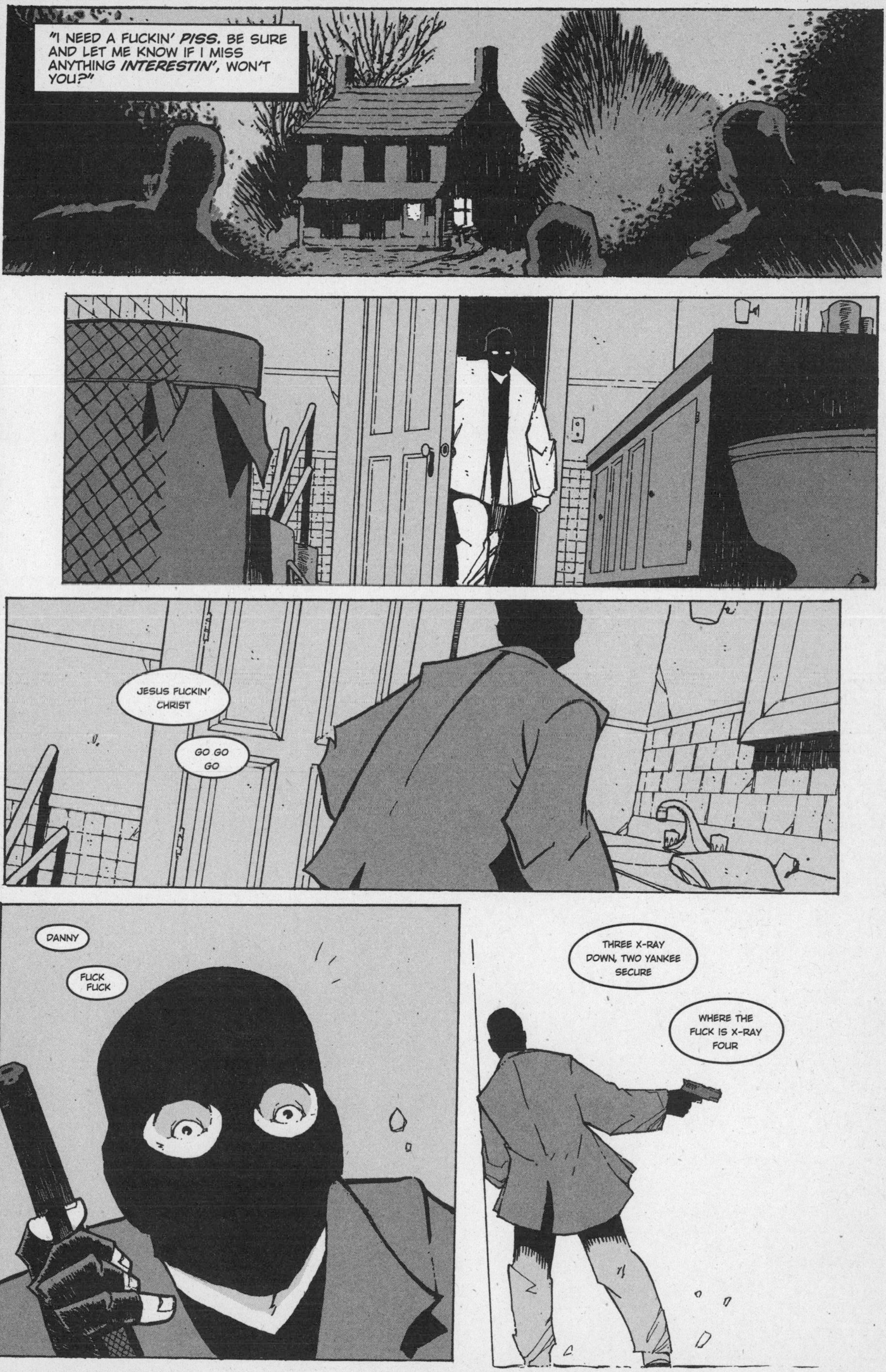
"I NEED A FUCKIN' *PISS.* BE SURE AND LET ME KNOW IF I MISS ANYTHING *INTERESTIN'*, WON'T YOU?"
JESUS FUCKIN' CHRIST
GO GO GO
DANNY
FUCK FUCK
THREE X-RAY DOWN, TWO YANKEE SECURE
WHERE THE FUCK IS X-RAY FOUR

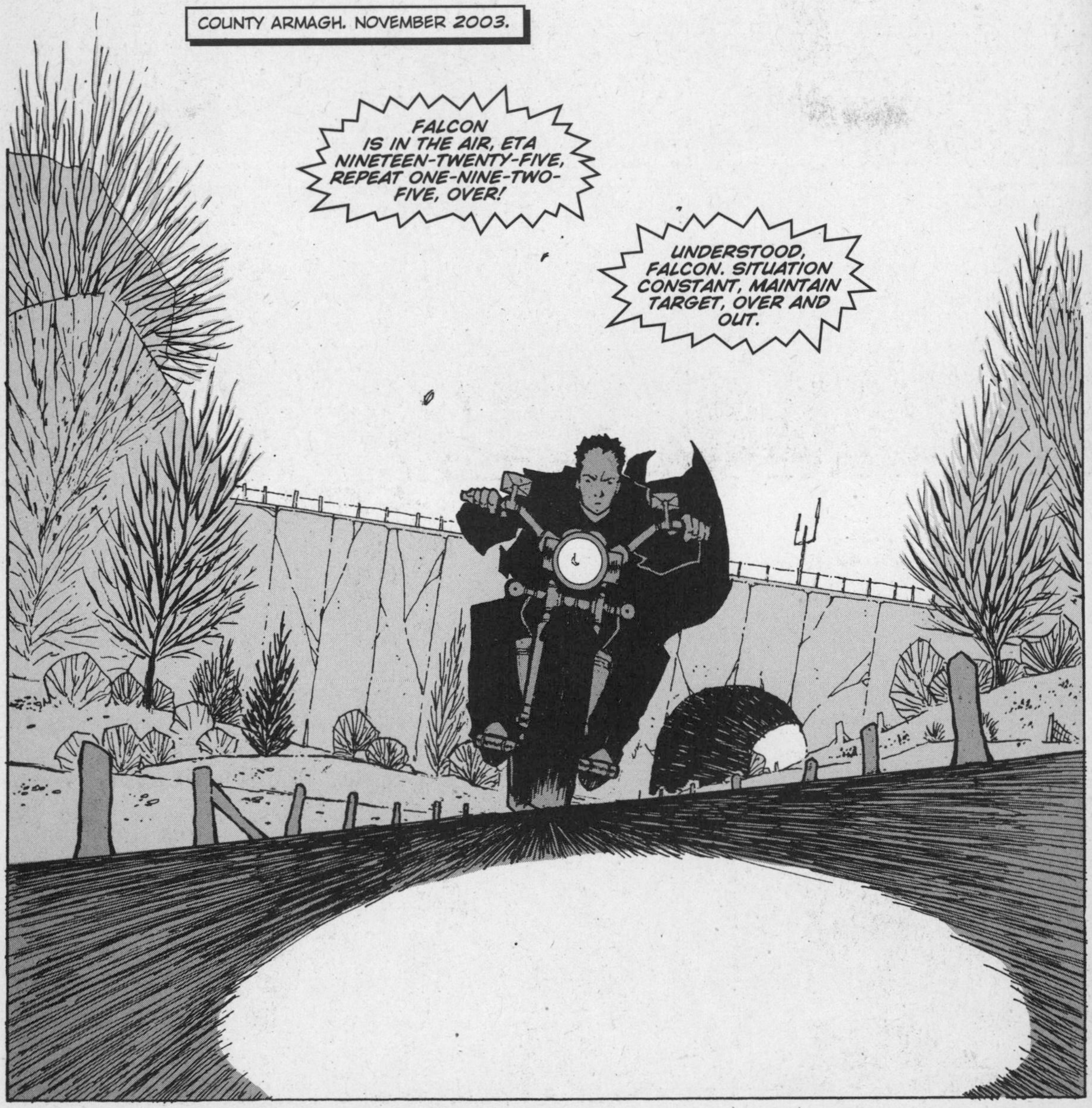
COUNTY ARMAGH. NOVEMBER 2003.
FALCON IS IN THE AIR, ETA NINETEEN-TWENTY-FIVE, REPEAT ONE-NINE-TWO-FIVE, OVER!
UNDERSTOOD, FALCON. SITUATION CONSTANT, MAINTAIN TARGET, OVER AND OUT.

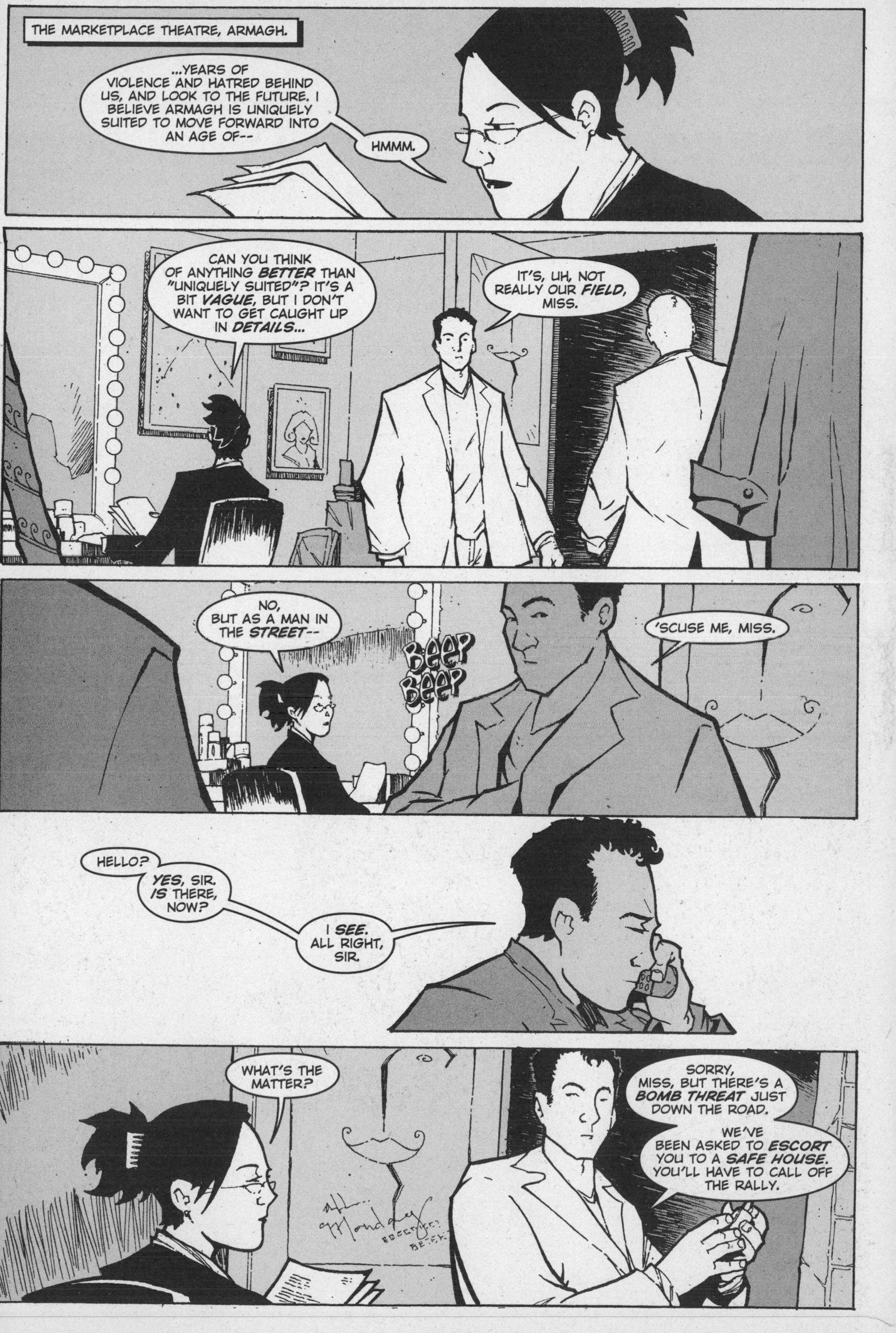
THE MARKETPLACE THEATRE, ARMAGH.
...YEARS OF VIOLENCE AND HATRED BEHIND US, AND LOOK TO THE FUTURE. I BELIEVE ARMAGH IS UNIQUELY SUITED TO MOVE FORWARD INTO AN AGE OF--
HMMM.
CAN YOU THINK OF ANYTHING BETTER THAN "UNIQUELY SUITED"? IT'S A BIT VAGUE, BUT I DON'T WANT TO GET CAUGHT UP IN DETAILS...
IT'S, UH, NOT REALLY OUR FIELD, MISS.
NO, BUT AS A MAN IN THE STREET--
BEEP BEEP
'SCUSE ME, MISS.
HELLO?
YES, SIR. IS THERE, NOW?
I SEE. ALL RIGHT, SIR.
WHAT'S THE MATTER?
SORRY, MISS, BUT THERE'S A BOMB THREAT JUST DOWN THE ROAD.
WE'VE BEEN ASKED TO ESCORT YOU TO A SAFE HOUSE. YOU'LL HAVE TO CALL OFF THE RALLY.

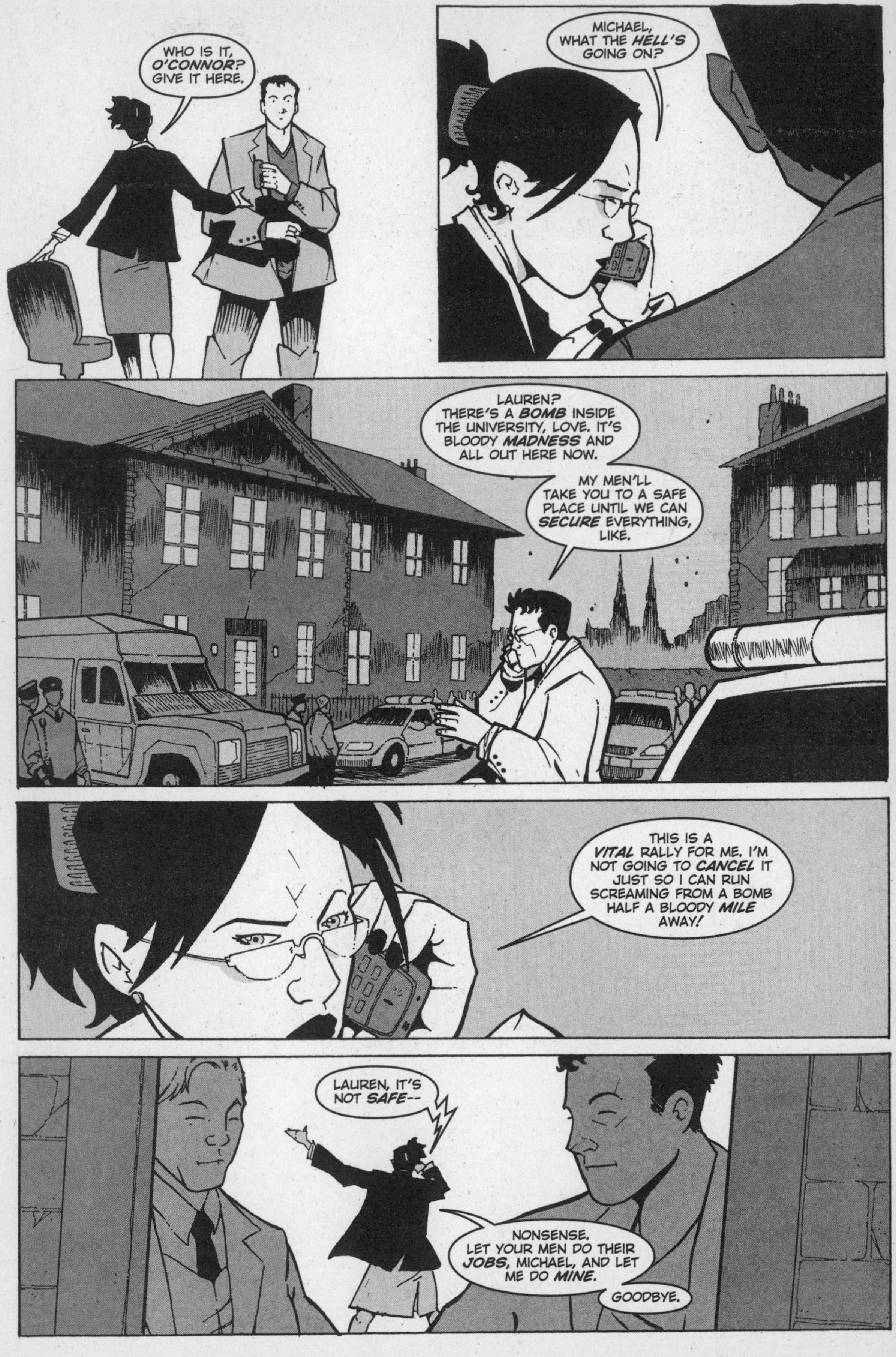
WHO IS IT, O'CONNOR? GIVE IT HERE.
MICHAEL, WHAT THE HELL'S GOING ON?
LAUREN? THERE'S A BOMB INSIDE THE UNIVERSITY, LOVE. IT'S BLOODY MADNESS AND ALL OUT HERE NOW.
MY MEN'LL TAKE YOU TO A SAFE PLACE UNTIL WE CAN SECURE EVERYTHING, LIKE.
THIS IS A VITAL RALLY FOR ME. I'M NOT GOING TO CANCEL IT JUST SO I CAN RUN SCREAMING FROM A BOMB HALF A BLOODY MILE AWAY!
LAUREN, IT'S NOT SAFE--
NONSENSE. LET YOUR MEN DO THEIR JOBS, MICHAEL, AND LET ME DO MINE.
GOODBYE.

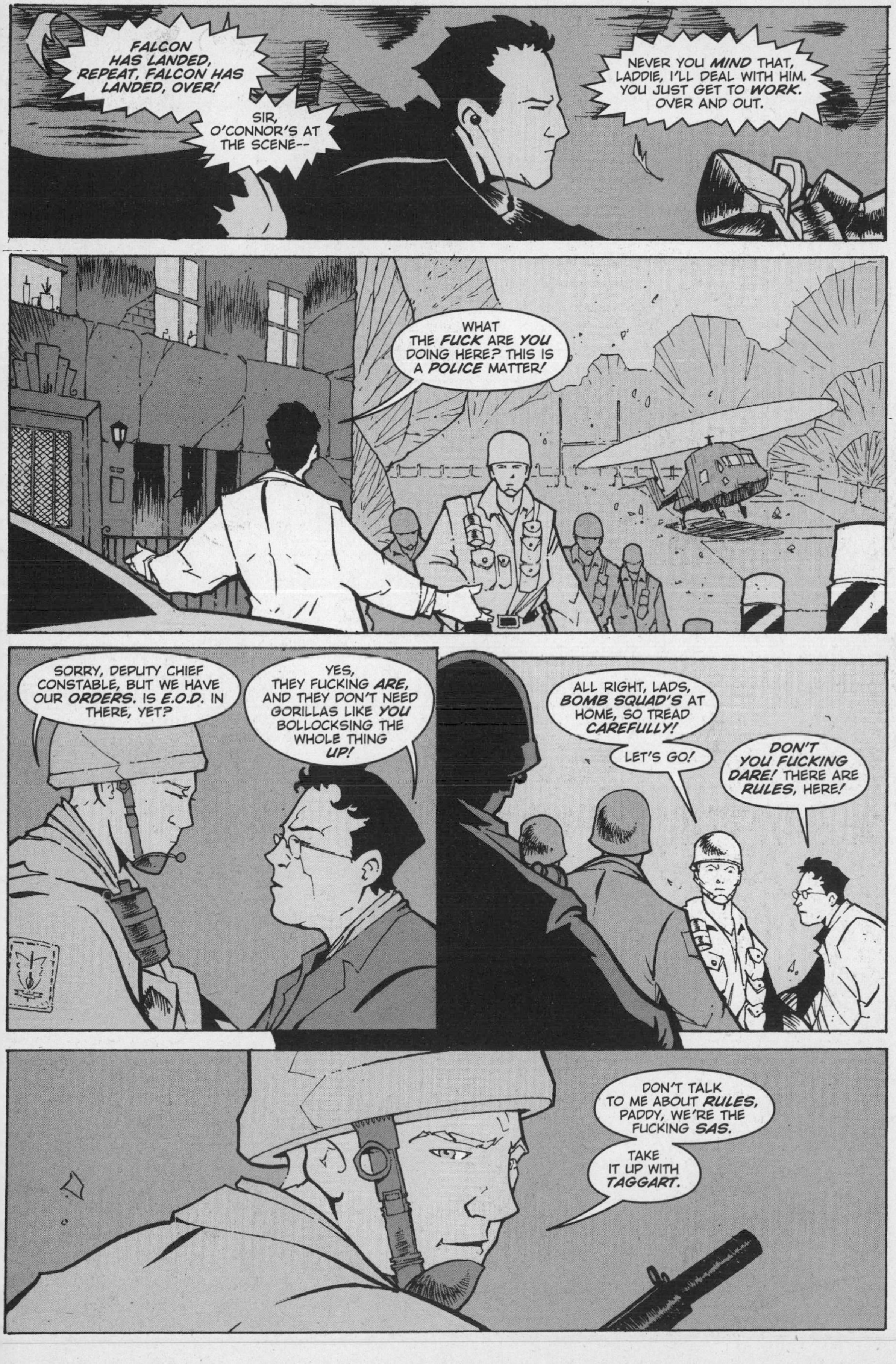
FALCON HAS LANDED, REPEAT, FALCON HAS LANDED, OVER!
SIR, O'CONNOR'S AT THE SCENE--
NEVER YOU MIND THAT, LADDIE, I'LL DEAL WITH HIM. YOU JUST GET TO WORK. OVER AND OUT.
WHAT THE FUCK ARE YOU DOING HERE? THIS IS A POLICE MATTER!
SORRY, DEPUTY CHIEF CONSTABLE, BUT WE HAVE OUR ORDERS. IS E.O.D. IN THERE, YET?
YES, THEY FUCKING ARE, AND THEY DON'T NEED GORILLAS LIKE YOU BOLLOCKSING THE WHOLE THING UP!
ALL RIGHT, LADS, BOMB SQUAD'S AT HOME, SO TREAD CAREFULLY!
LET'S GO!
DON'T YOU FUCKING DARE! THERE ARE RULES, HERE!
DON'T TALK TO ME ABOUT RULES, PADDY, WE'RE THE FUCKING SAS.
TAKE IT UP WITH TAGGART.

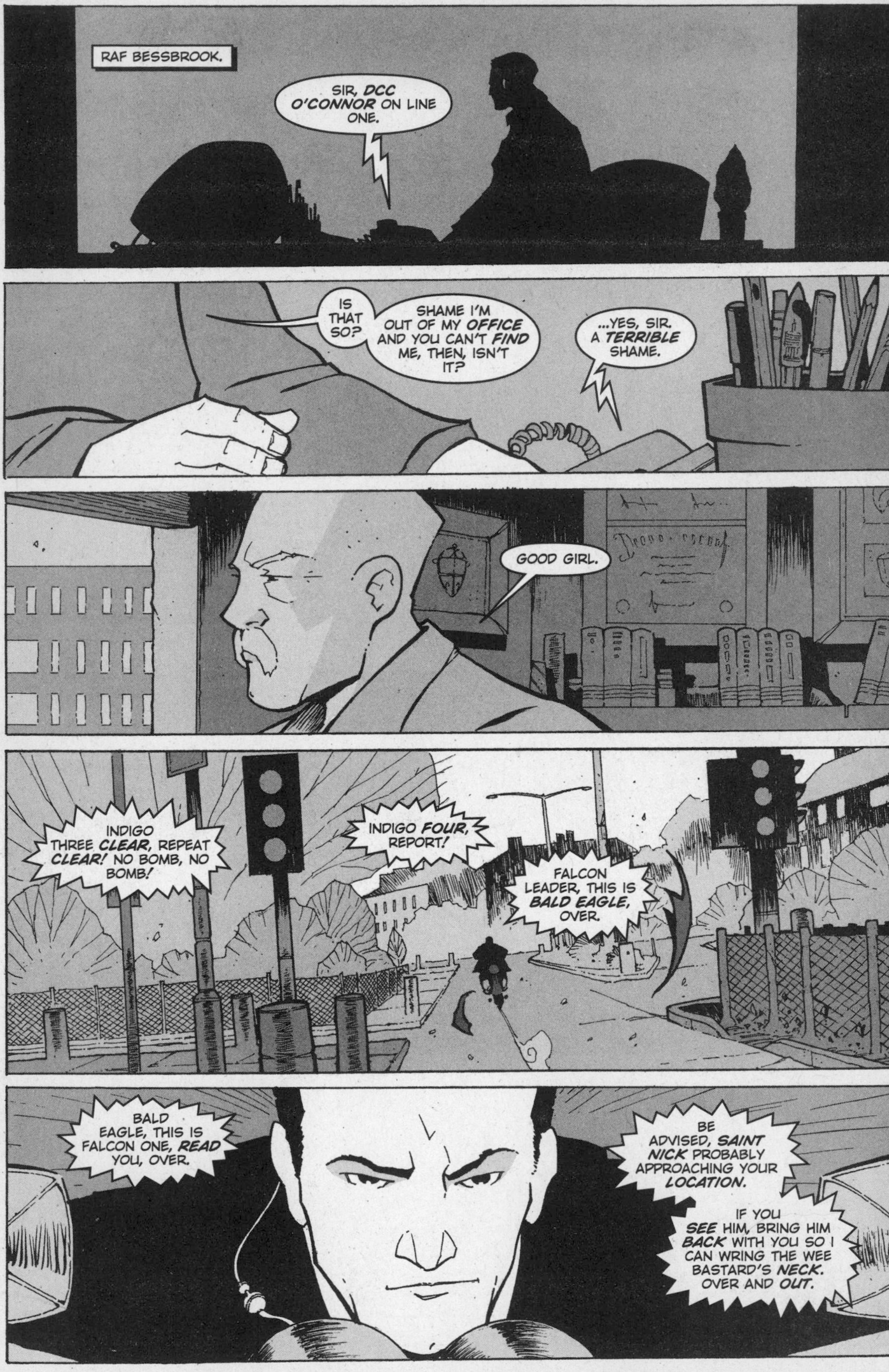
RAF BESSBROOK.
SIR, DCC O'CONNOR ON LINE ONE.
IS THAT SO?
SHAME I'M OUT OF MY OFFICE AND YOU CAN'T FIND ME, THEN, ISN'T IT?
...YES, SIR. A TERRIBLE SHAME.
GOOD GIRL.
INDIGO THREE CLEAR, REPEAT CLEAR! NO BOMB, NO BOMB!
INDIGO FOUR, REPORT!
FALCON LEADER, THIS IS BALD EAGLE, OVER.
BALD EAGLE, THIS IS FALCON ONE, READ YOU, OVER.
BE ADVISED, SAINT NICK PROBABLY APPROACHING YOUR LOCATION.
IF YOU SEE HIM, BRING HIM BACK WITH YOU SO I CAN WRING THE WEE BASTARD'S NECK. OVER AND OUT.

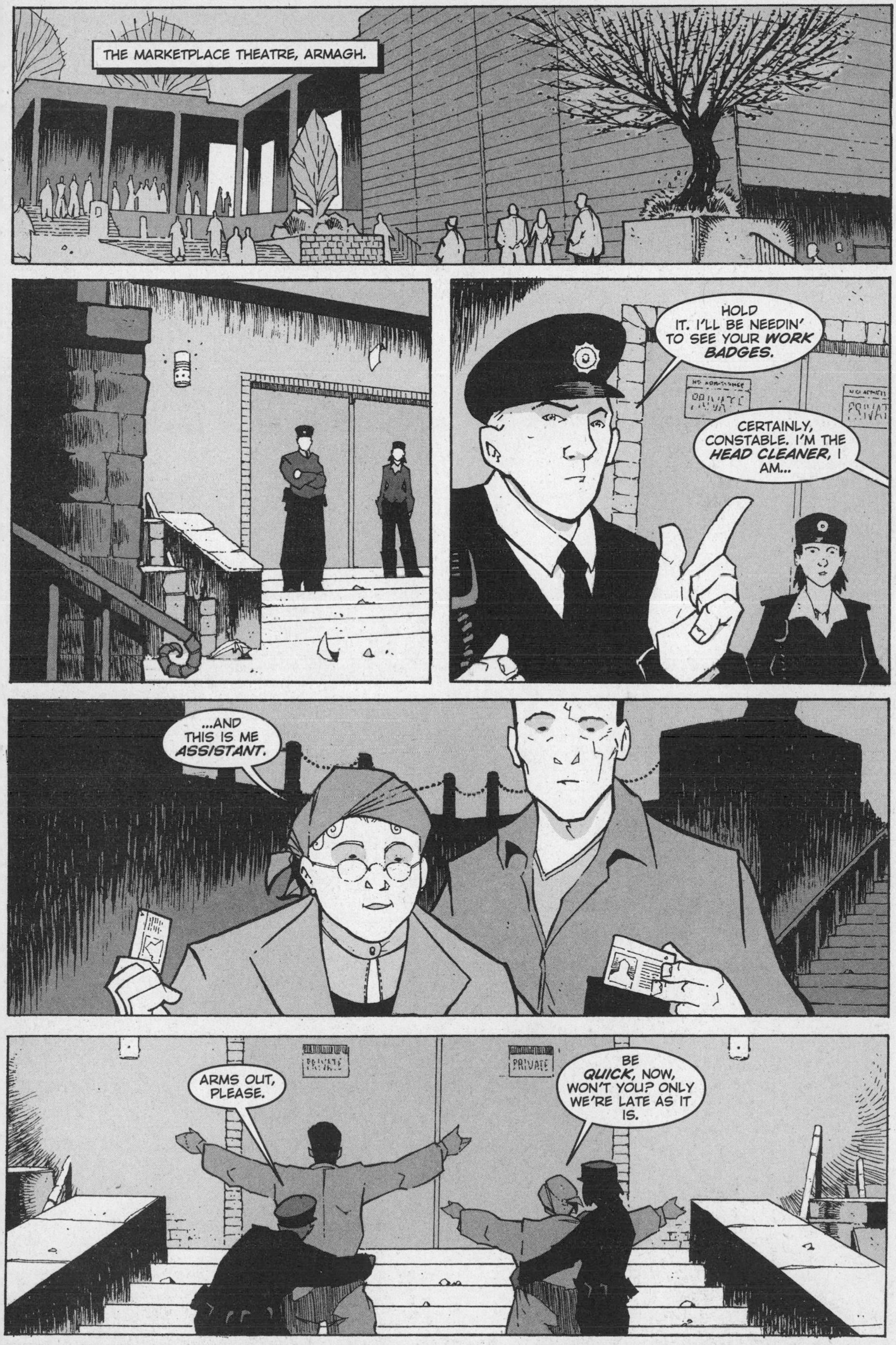
THE MARKETPLACE THEATRE, ARMAGH.
HOLD IT. I'LL BE NEEDIN' TO SEE YOUR *WORK BADGES.*
CERTAINLY, CONSTABLE. I'M THE *HEAD CLEANER,* I AM...
...AND THIS IS ME *ASSISTANT.*
PRIVATE
PRIVATE
ARMS OUT, PLEASE.
BE *QUICK,* NOW, WON'T YOU? ONLY WE'RE LATE AS IT IS.

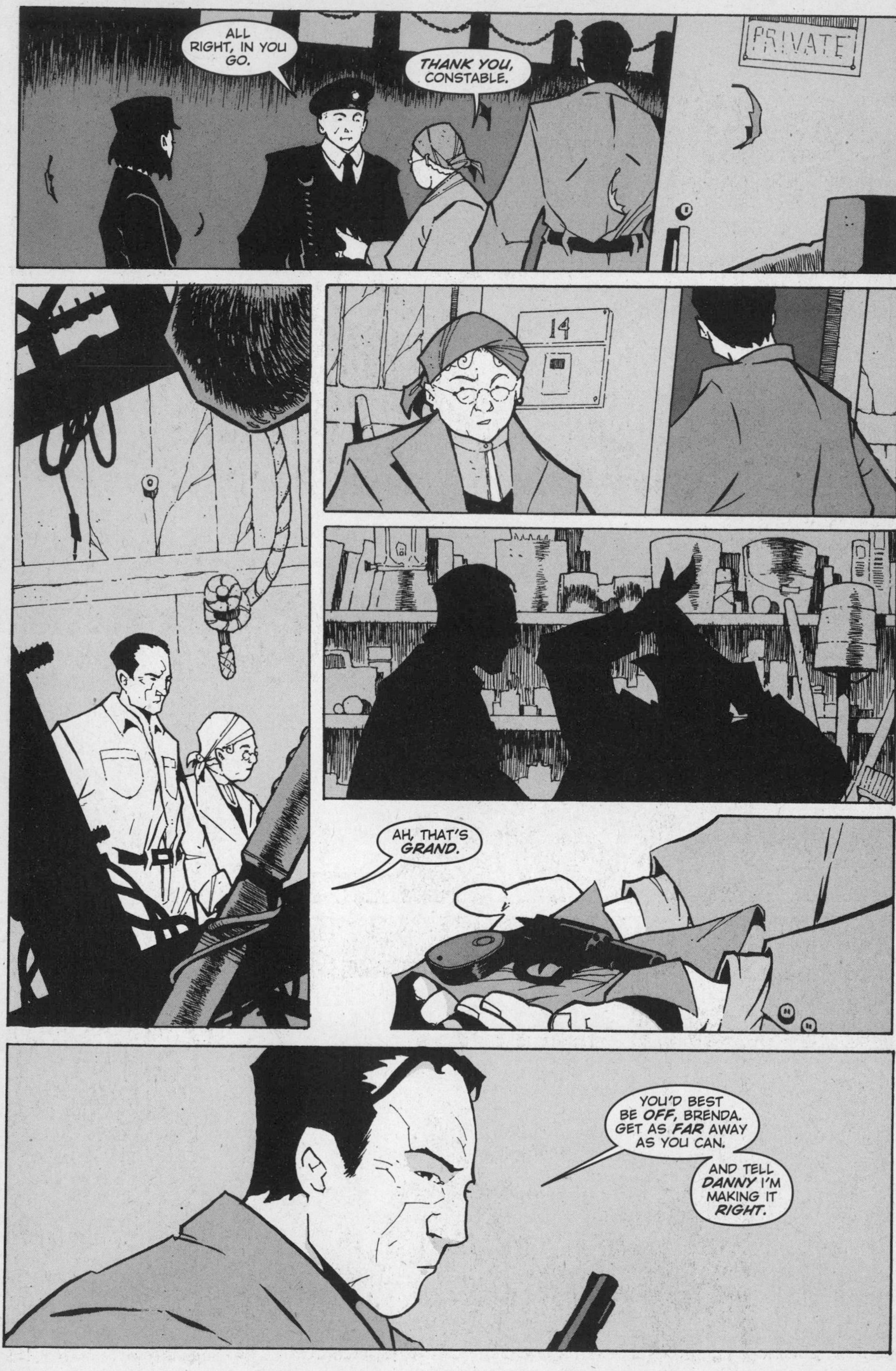
ALL RIGHT, IN YOU GO.
THANK YOU, CONSTABLE.
PRIVATE
14
AH, THAT'S GRAND.
YOU'D BEST BE OFF, BRENDA. GET AS FAR AWAY AS YOU CAN.
AND TELL DANNY I'M MAKING IT RIGHT.

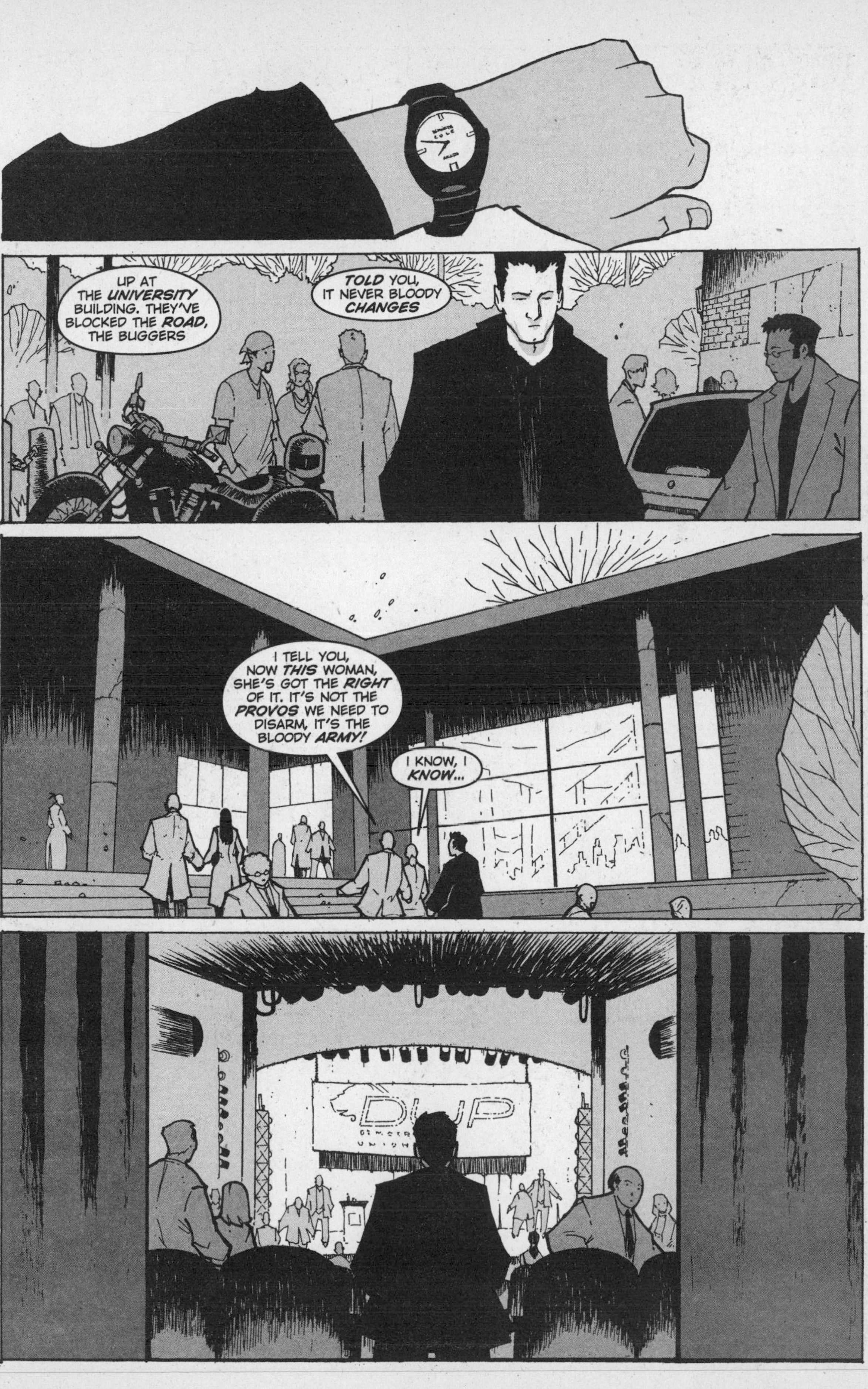
UP AT THE *UNIVERSITY* BUILDING. THEY'VE BLOCKED THE *ROAD*, THE BUGGERS
TOLD YOU, IT NEVER BLOODY *CHANGES*
I TELL YOU, NOW *THIS* WOMAN, SHE'S GOT THE *RIGHT* OF IT. IT'S NOT THE *PROVOS* WE NEED TO DISARM, IT'S THE BLOODY *ARMY!*
I KNOW, I *KNOW*...
DUP

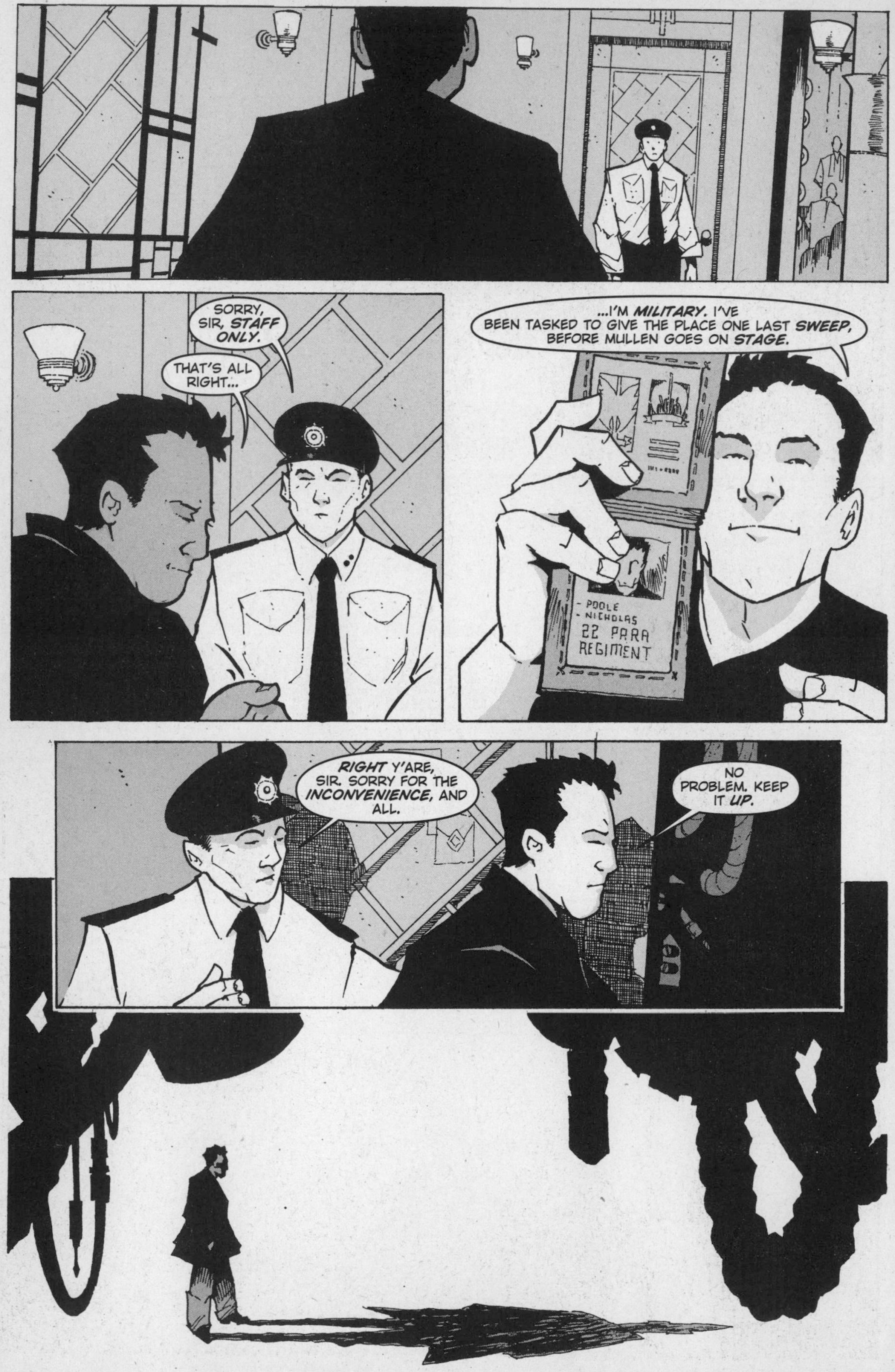
SORRY, SIR, STAFF ONLY.
THAT'S ALL RIGHT...
...I'M MILITARY. I'VE BEEN TASKED TO GIVE THE PLACE ONE LAST SWEEP, BEFORE MULLEN GOES ON STAGE.
POOLE
NICHOLAS
22 PARA
REGIMENT
RIGHT Y'ARE, SIR. SORRY FOR THE INCONVENIENCE, AND ALL.
NO PROBLEM. KEEP IT UP.

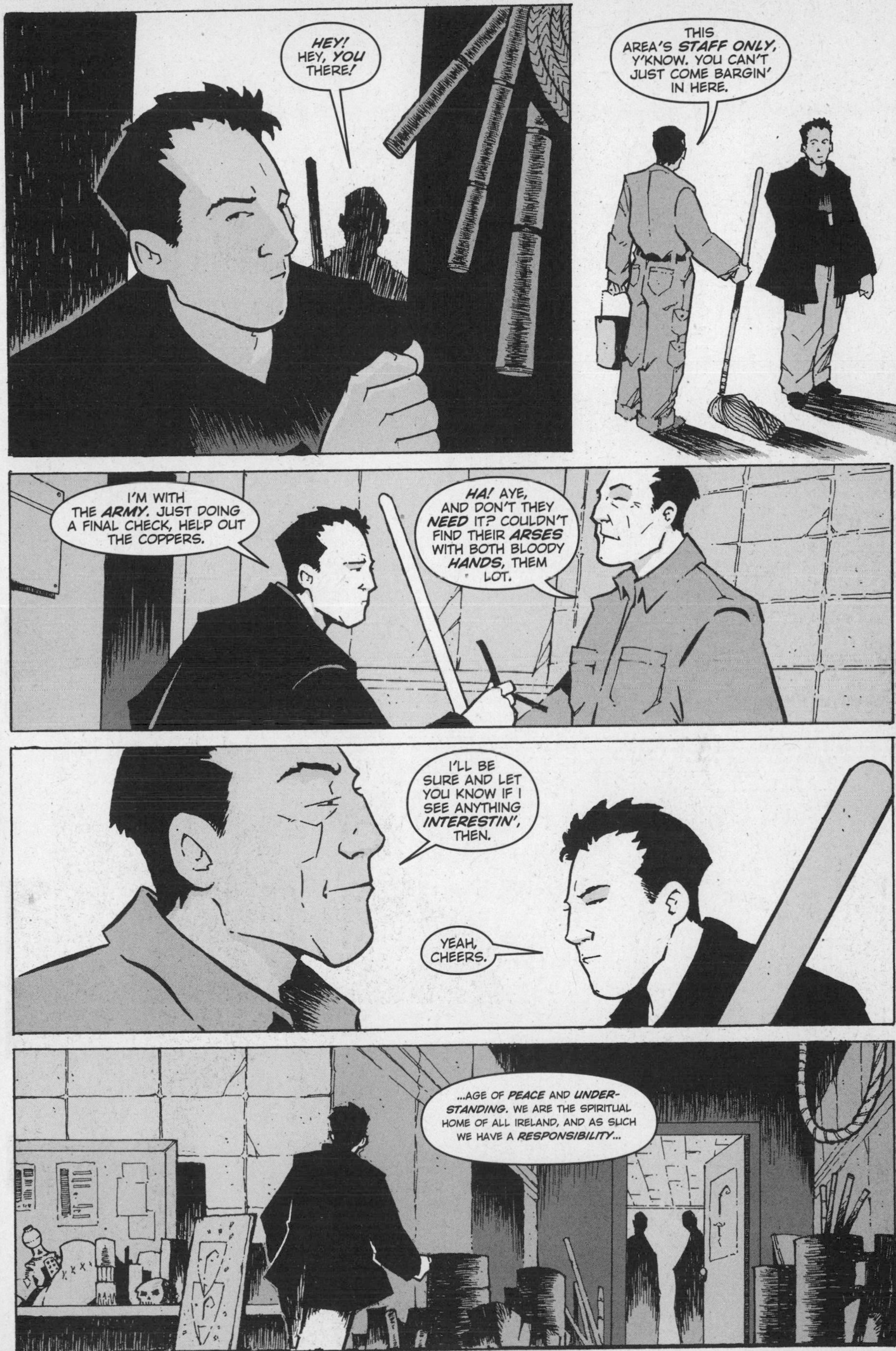
HEY! HEY, YOU THERE!
THIS AREA'S STAFF ONLY, Y'KNOW. YOU CAN'T JUST COME BARGIN' IN HERE.
I'M WITH THE ARMY. JUST DOING A FINAL CHECK, HELP OUT THE COPPERS.
HA! AYE, AND DON'T THEY NEED IT? COULDN'T FIND THEIR ARSES WITH BOTH BLOODY HANDS, THEM LOT.
I'LL BE SURE AND LET YOU KNOW IF I SEE ANYTHING INTERESTIN', THEN.
YEAH, CHEERS.
...AGE OF PEACE AND UNDER-STANDING. WE ARE THE SPIRITUAL HOME OF ALL IRELAND, AND AS SUCH WE HAVE A RESPONSIBILITY...

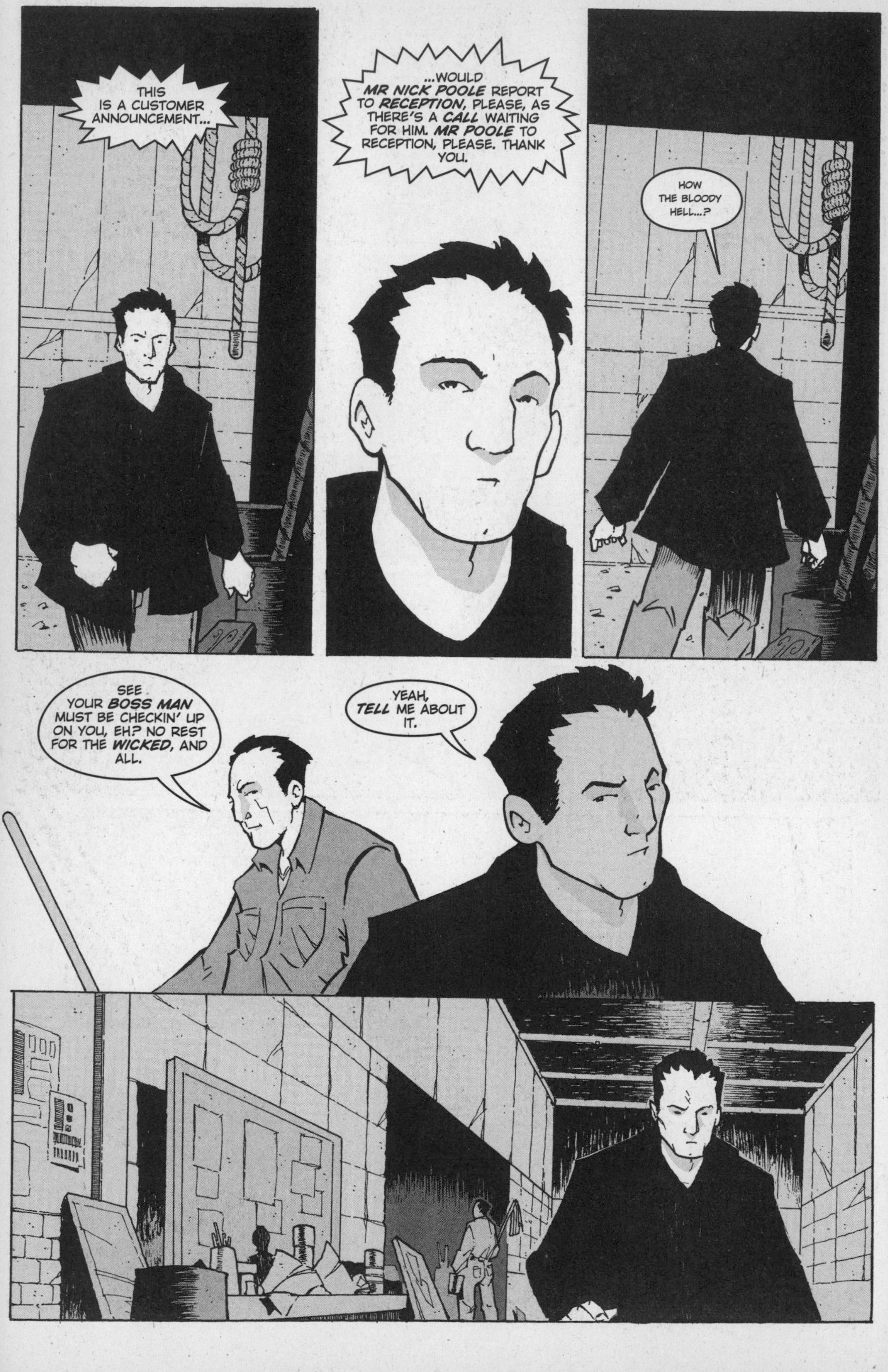
THIS IS A CUSTOMER ANNOUNCEMENT...
...WOULD MR NICK POOLE REPORT TO RECEPTION, PLEASE, AS THERE'S A CALL WAITING FOR HIM. MR POOLE TO RECEPTION, PLEASE. THANK YOU.
HOW THE BLOODY HELL...?
SEE YOUR BOSS MAN MUST BE CHECKIN' UP ON YOU, EH? NO REST FOR THE WICKED, AND ALL.
YEAH, TELL ME ABOUT IT.

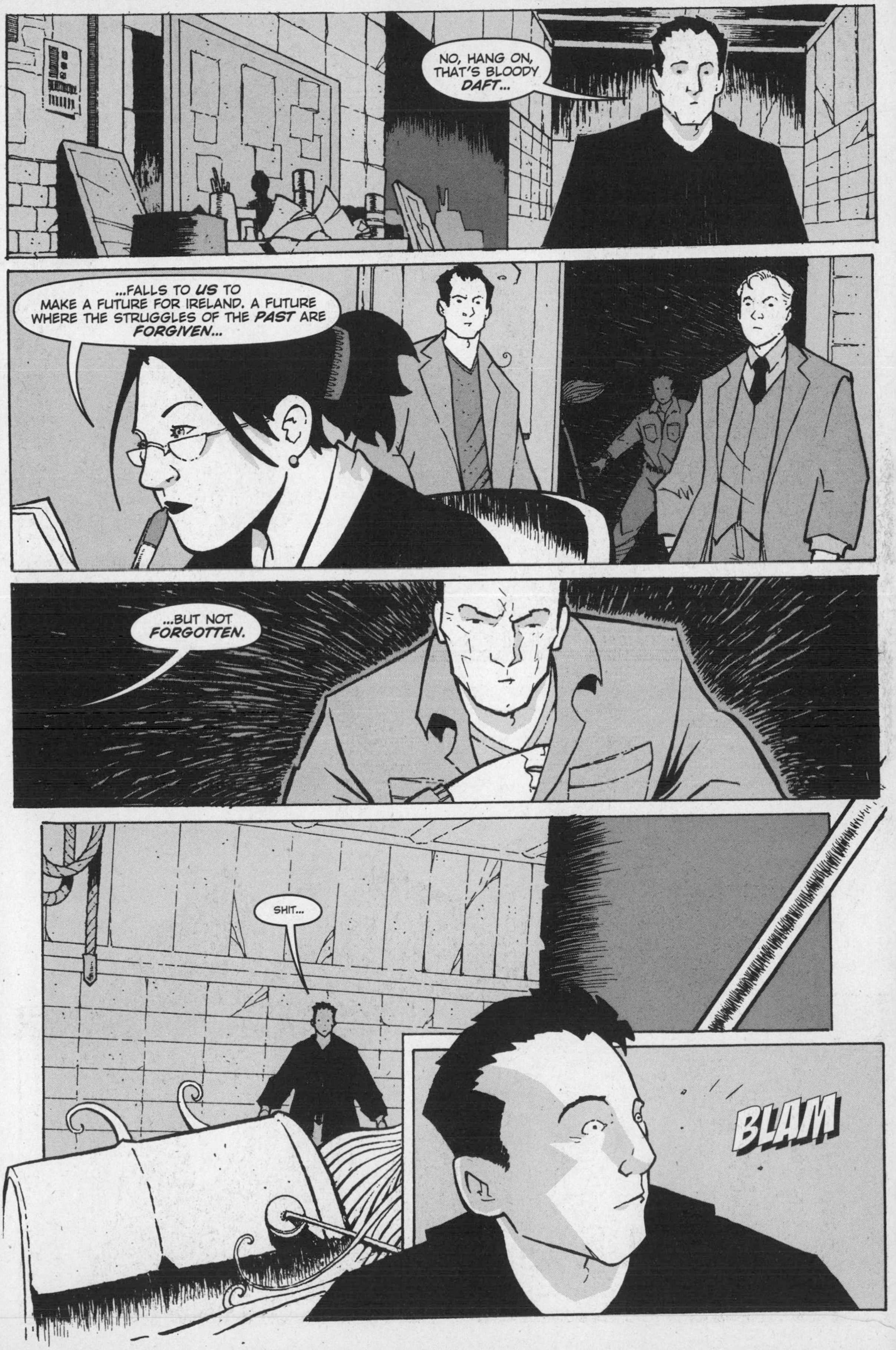
NO, HANG ON, THAT'S BLOODY DAFT...
...FALLS TO US TO MAKE A FUTURE FOR IRELAND. A FUTURE WHERE THE STRUGGLES OF THE PAST ARE FORGIVEN...
...BUT NOT FORGOTTEN.
SHIT...
BLAM

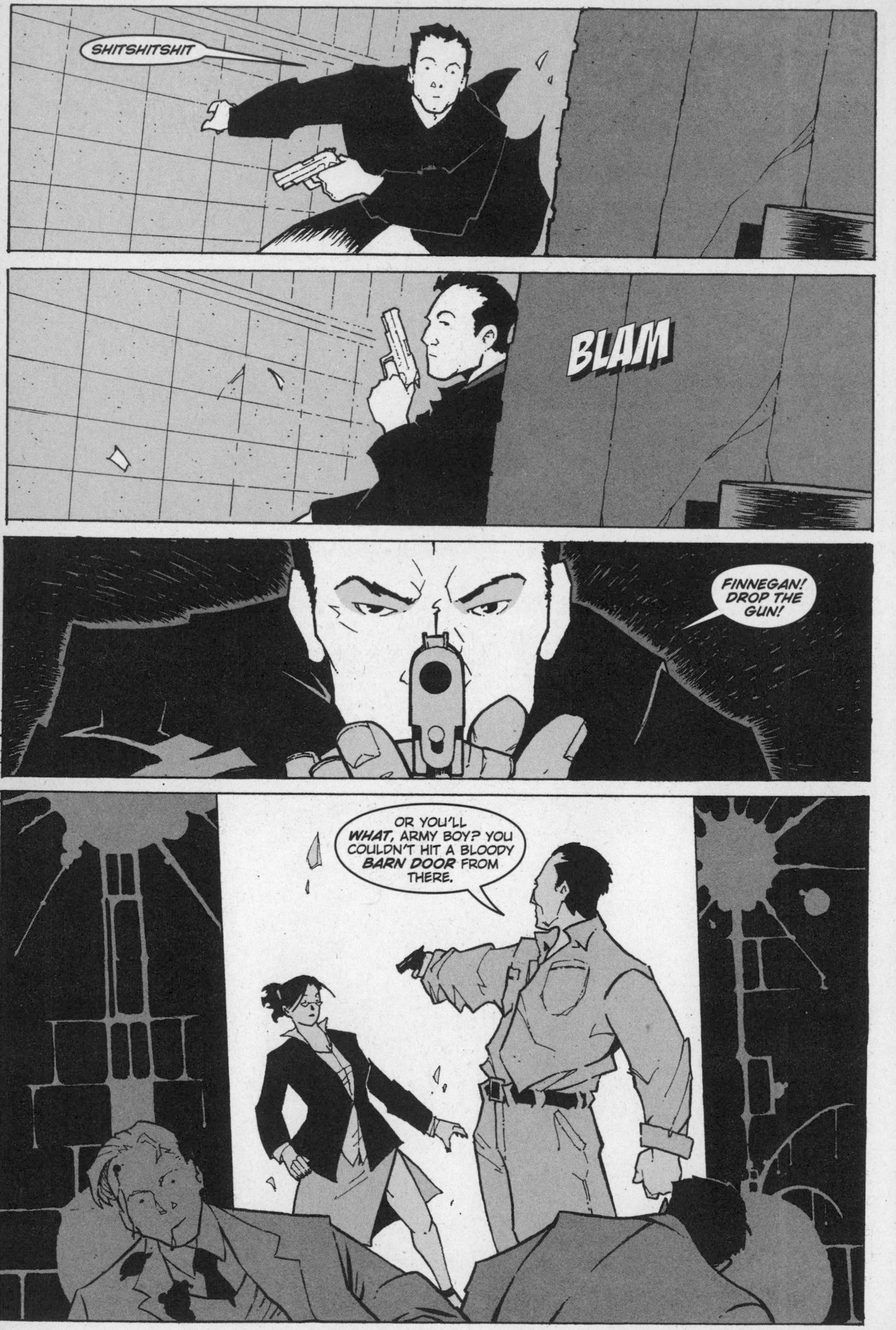
SHITSHITSHIT
BLAM
FINNEGAN! DROP THE GUN!
OR YOU'LL WHAT, ARMY BOY? YOU COULDN'T HIT A BLOODY BARN DOOR FROM THERE.

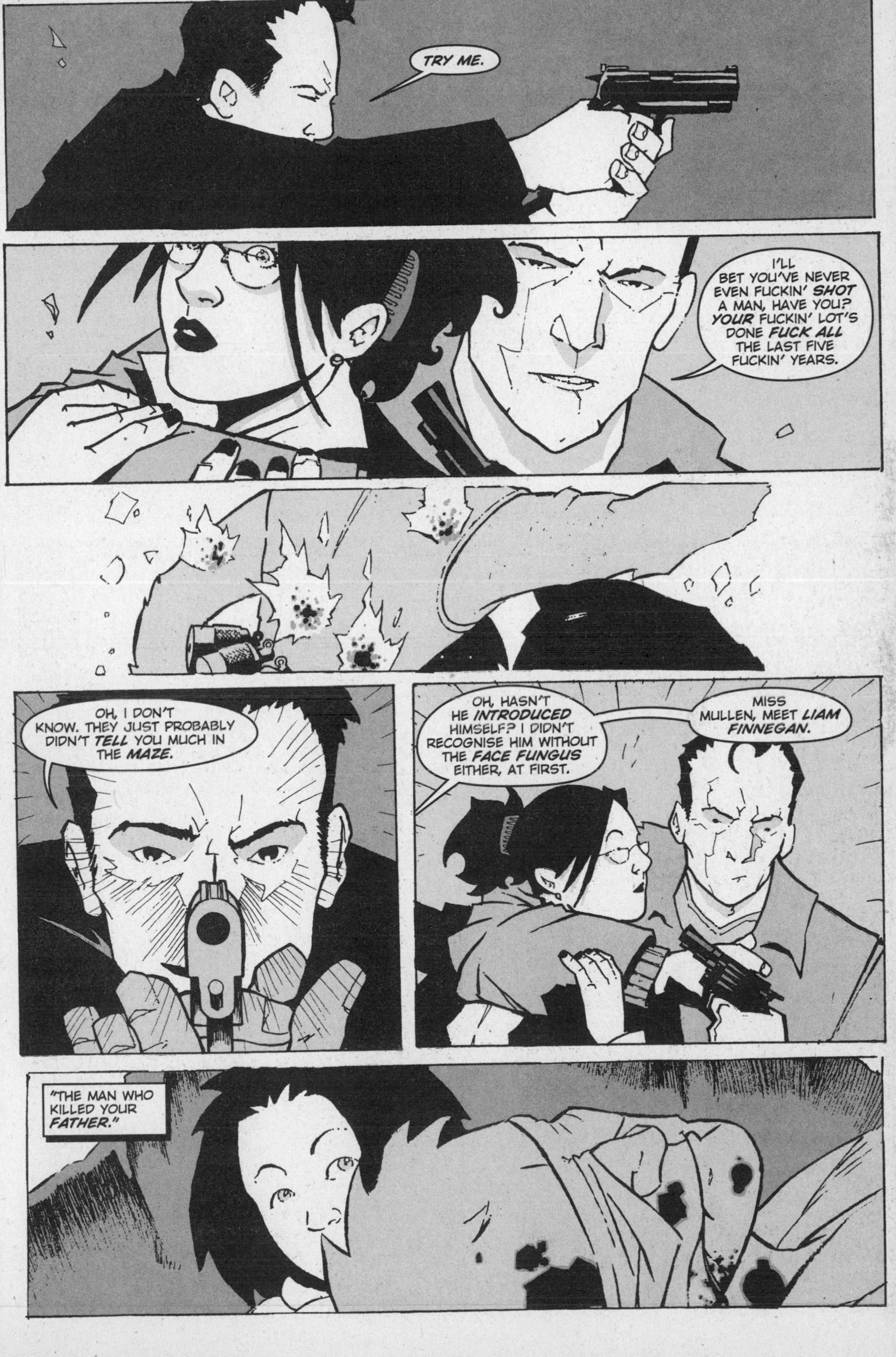
TRY ME.
I'LL BET YOU'VE NEVER EVEN FUCKIN' SHOT A MAN, HAVE YOU? YOUR FUCKIN' LOT'S DONE FUCK ALL THE LAST FIVE FUCKIN' YEARS.
OH, I DON'T KNOW. THEY JUST PROBABLY DIDN'T TELL YOU MUCH IN THE MAZE.
OH, HASN'T HE INTRODUCED HIMSELF? I DIDN'T RECOGNISE HIM WITHOUT THE FACE FUNGUS EITHER, AT FIRST.
MISS MULLEN, MEET LIAM FINNEGAN.
"THE MAN WHO KILLED YOUR FATHER."

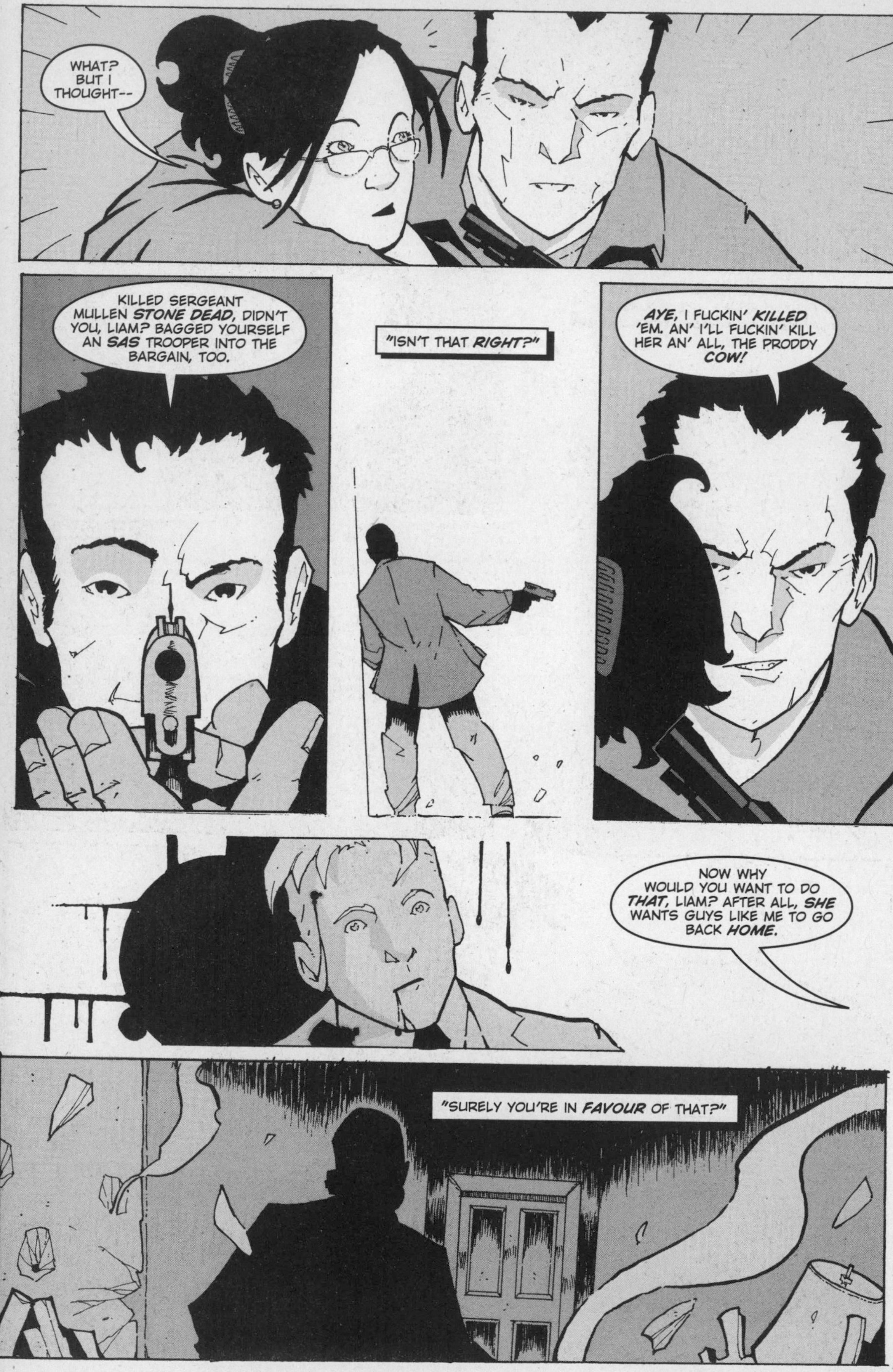
WHAT? BUT I THOUGHT--
KILLED SERGEANT MULLEN STONE DEAD, DIDN'T YOU, LIAM? BAGGED YOURSELF AN SAS TROOPER INTO THE BARGAIN, TOO.
"ISN'T THAT RIGHT?"
AYE, I FUCKIN' KILLED 'EM. AN' I'LL FUCKIN' KILL HER AN' ALL, THE PRODDY COW!
NOW WHY WOULD YOU WANT TO DO THAT, LIAM? AFTER ALL, SHE WANTS GUYS LIKE ME TO GO BACK HOME.
"SURELY YOU'RE IN FAVOUR OF THAT?"

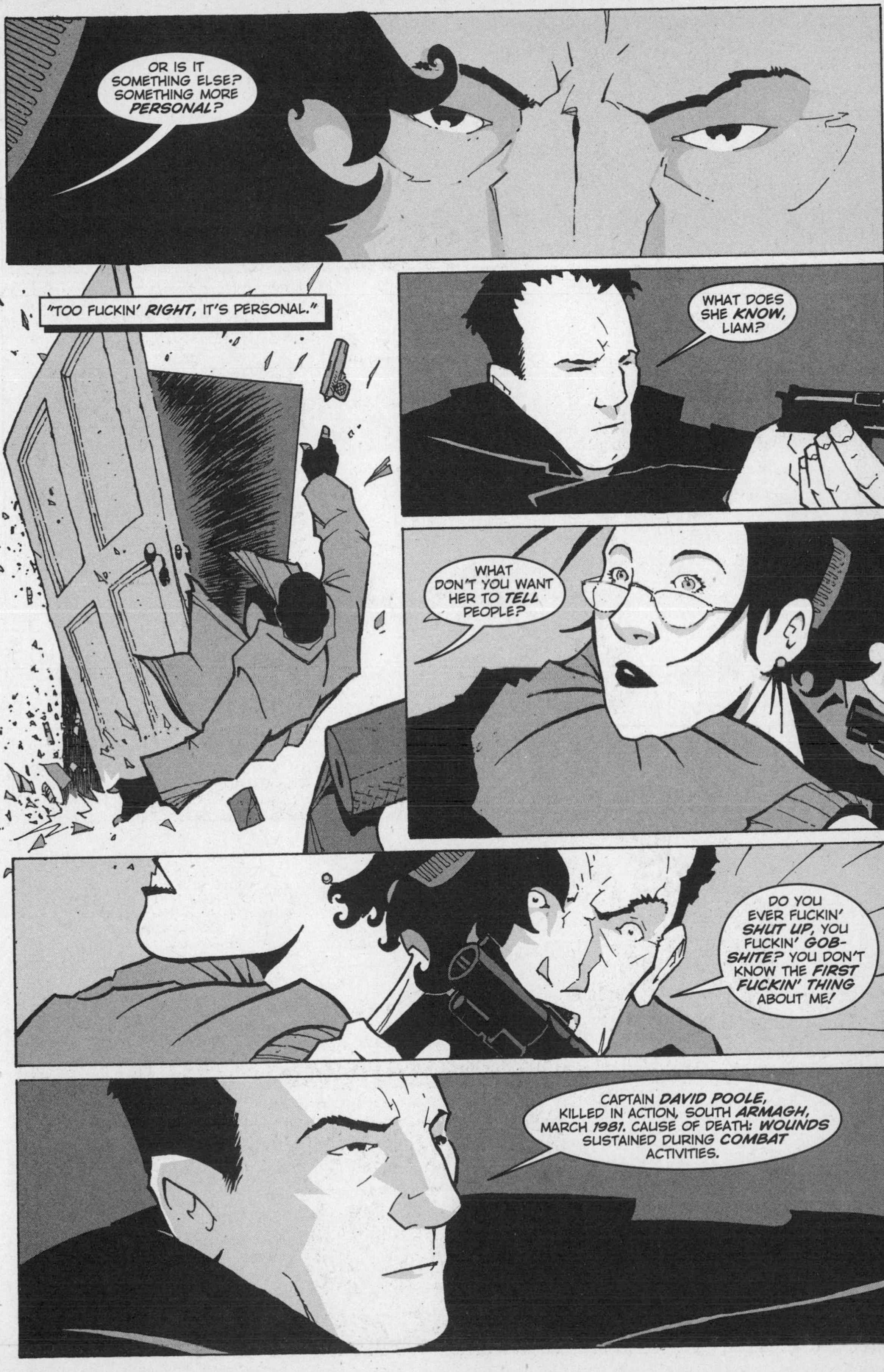

OR IS IT SOMETHING ELSE? SOMETHING MORE PERSONAL?
"TOO FUCKIN' RIGHT, IT'S PERSONAL."
WHAT DOES SHE KNOW, LIAM?
WHAT DON'T YOU WANT HER TO TELL PEOPLE?
DO YOU EVER FUCKIN' SHUT UP, YOU FUCKIN' GOB-SHITE? YOU DON'T KNOW THE FIRST FUCKIN' THING ABOUT ME!
CAPTAIN DAVID POOLE, KILLED IN ACTION, SOUTH ARMAGH, MARCH 1981. CAUSE OF DEATH: WOUNDS SUSTAINED DURING COMBAT ACTIVITIES.

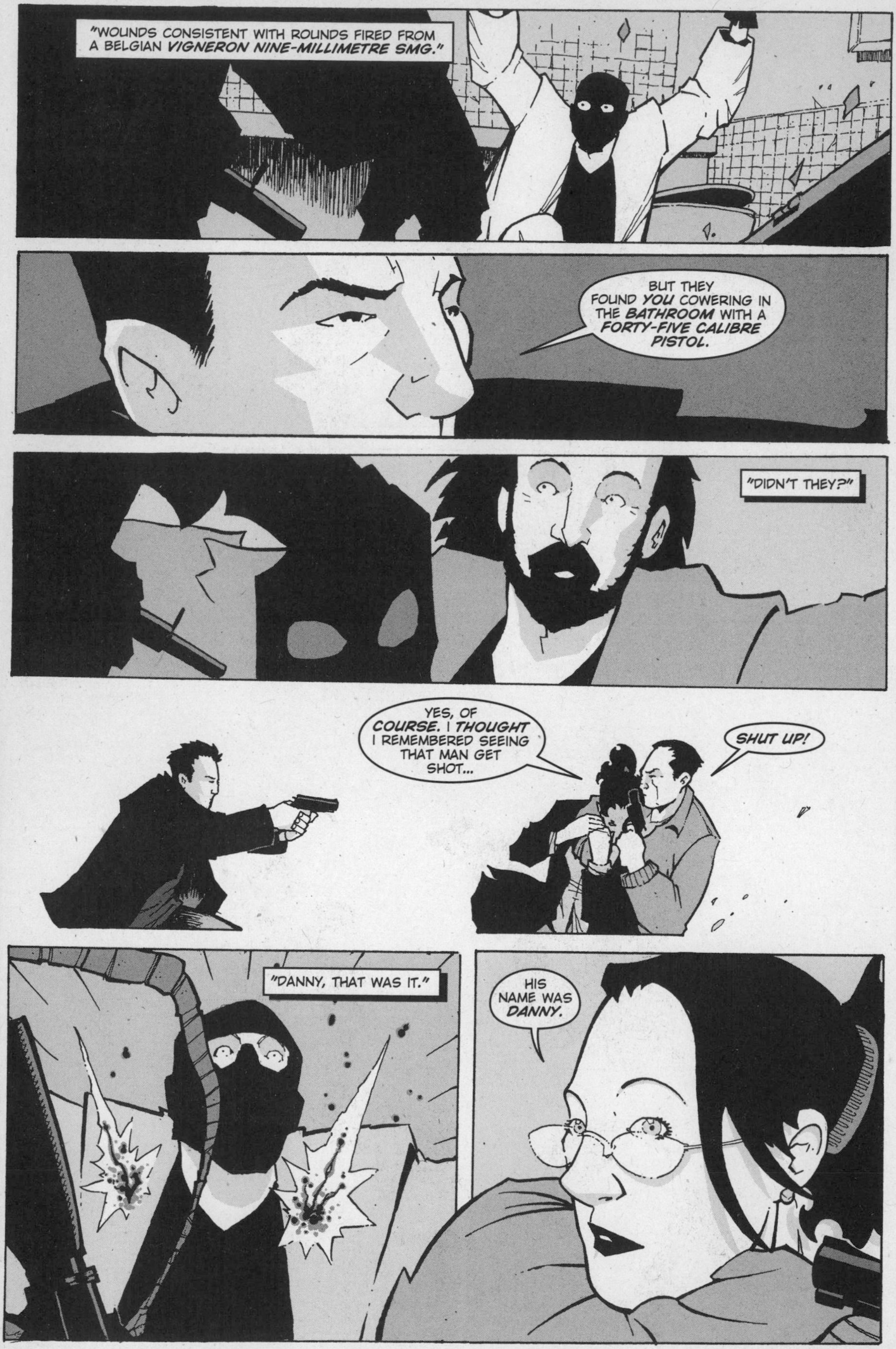
"WOUNDS CONSISTENT WITH ROUNDS FIRED FROM A BELGIAN VIGNERON NINE-MILLIMETRE SMG."
BUT THEY FOUND YOU COWERING IN THE BATHROOM WITH A FORTY-FIVE CALIBRE PISTOL.
"DIDN'T THEY?"
YES, OF COURSE. I THOUGHT I REMEMBERED SEEING THAT MAN GET SHOT...
SHUT UP!
"DANNY, THAT WAS IT."
HIS NAME WAS DANNY.

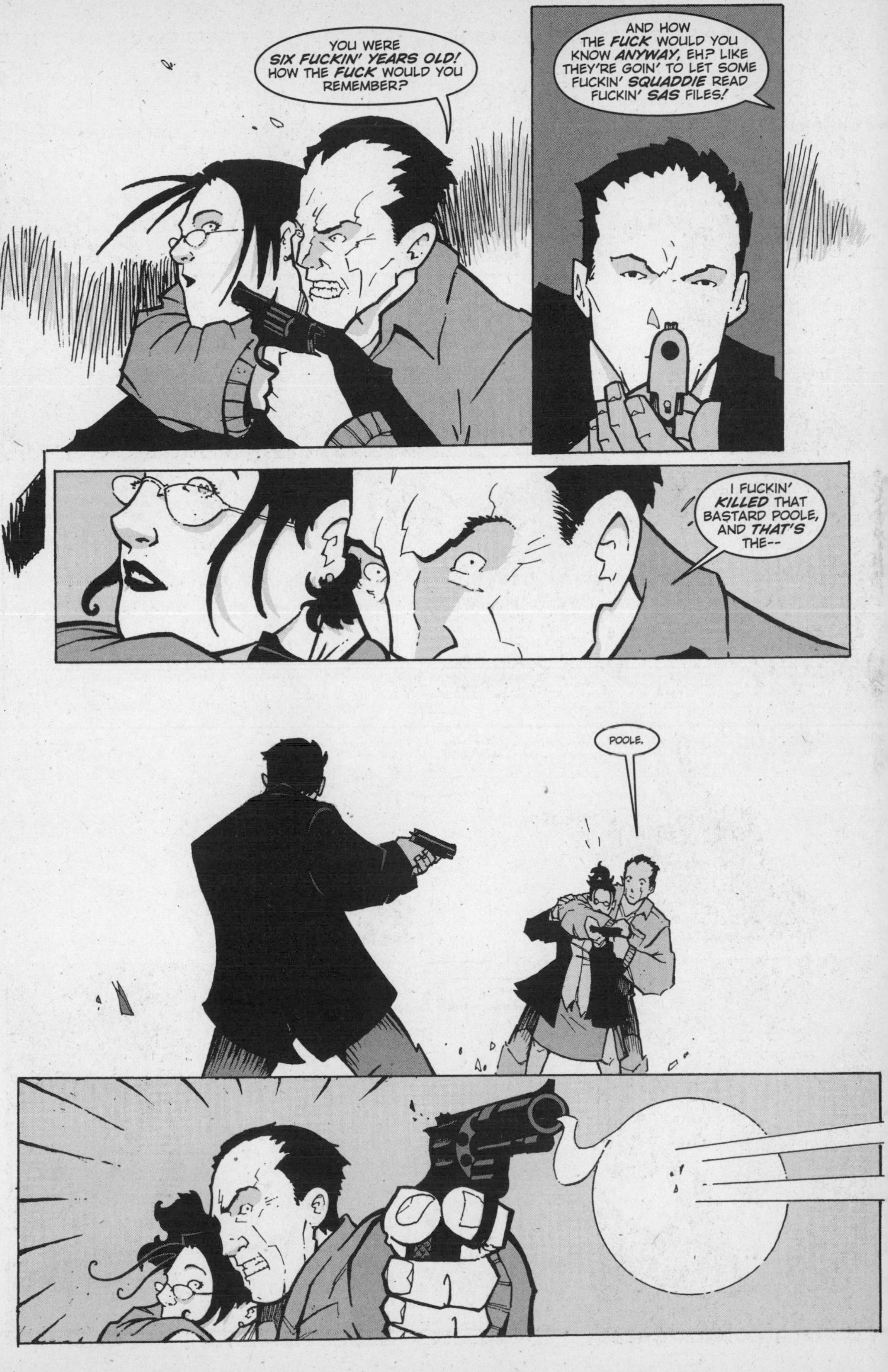
YOU WERE SIX FUCKIN' YEARS OLD! HOW THE FUCK WOULD YOU REMEMBER?
AND HOW THE FUCK WOULD YOU KNOW ANYWAY, EH? LIKE THEY'RE GOIN' TO LET SOME FUCKIN' SQUADDIE READ FUCKIN' SAS FILES!
I FUCKIN' KILLED THAT BASTARD POOLE, AND THAT'S THE--
POOLE.

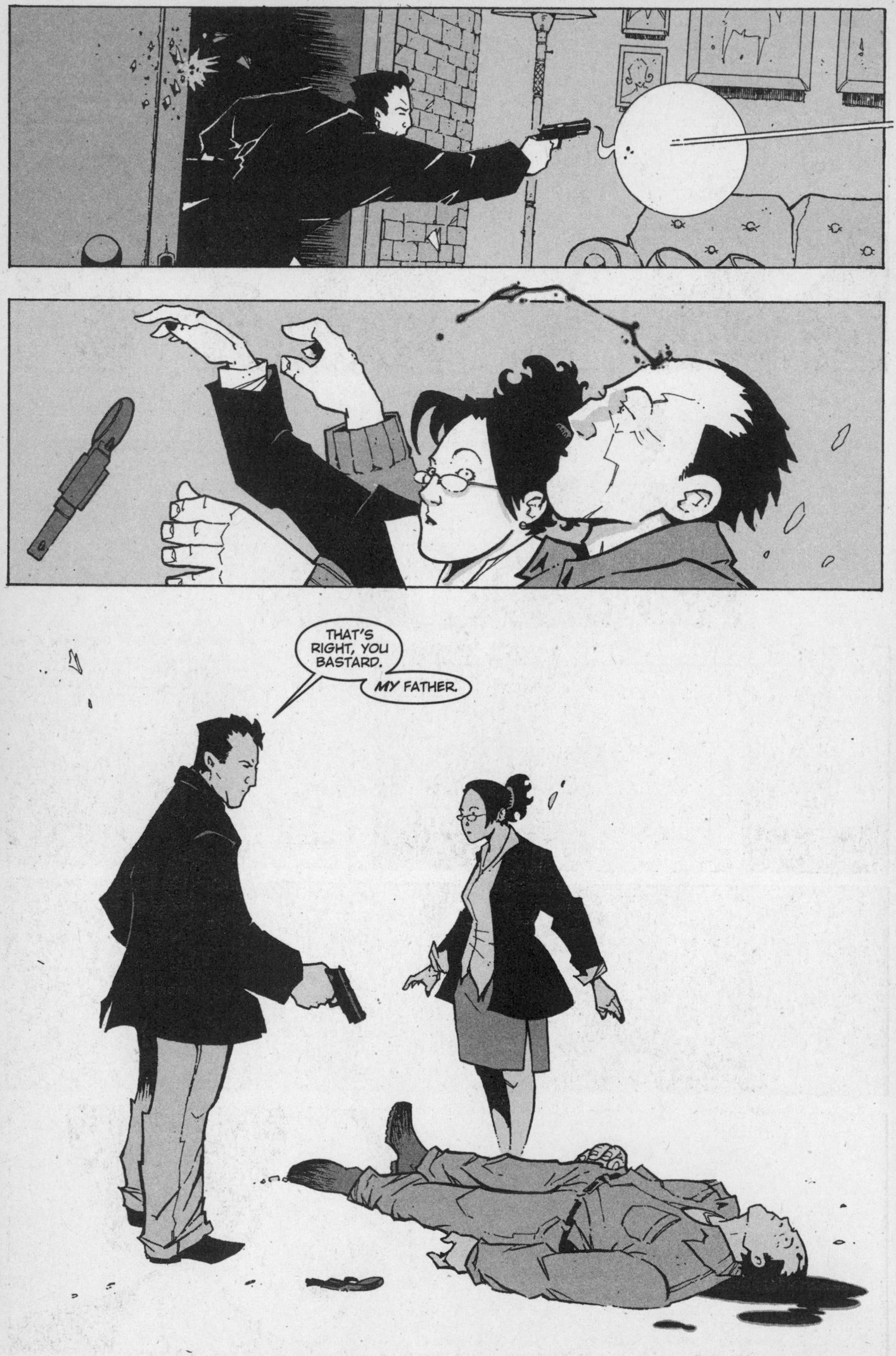
THAT'S RIGHT, YOU BASTARD.
MY FATHER.

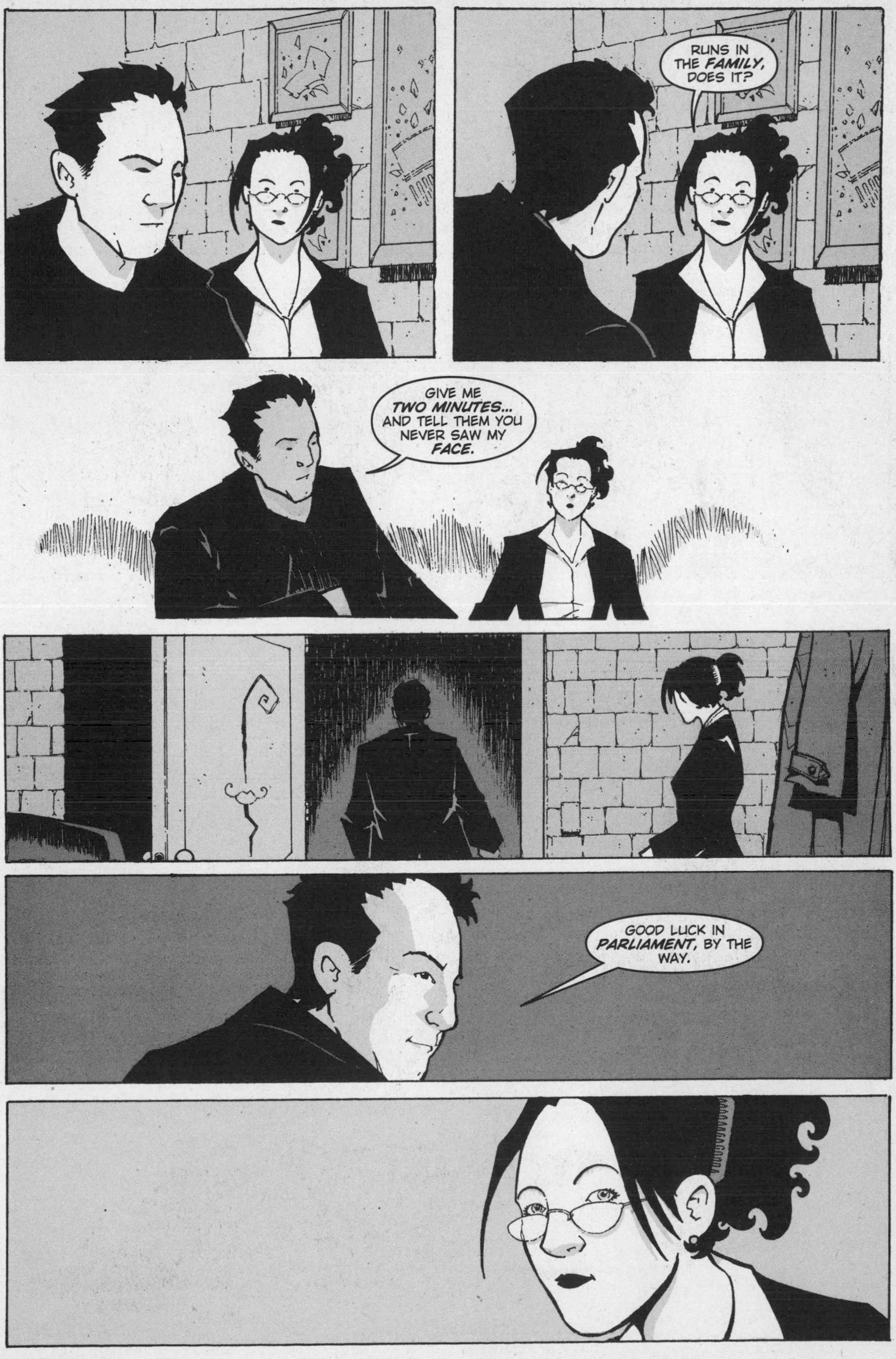
RUNS IN THE FAMILY, DOES IT?
GIVE ME TWO MINUTES... AND TELL THEM YOU NEVER SAW MY FACE.
GOOD LUCK IN PARLIAMENT, BY THE WAY.

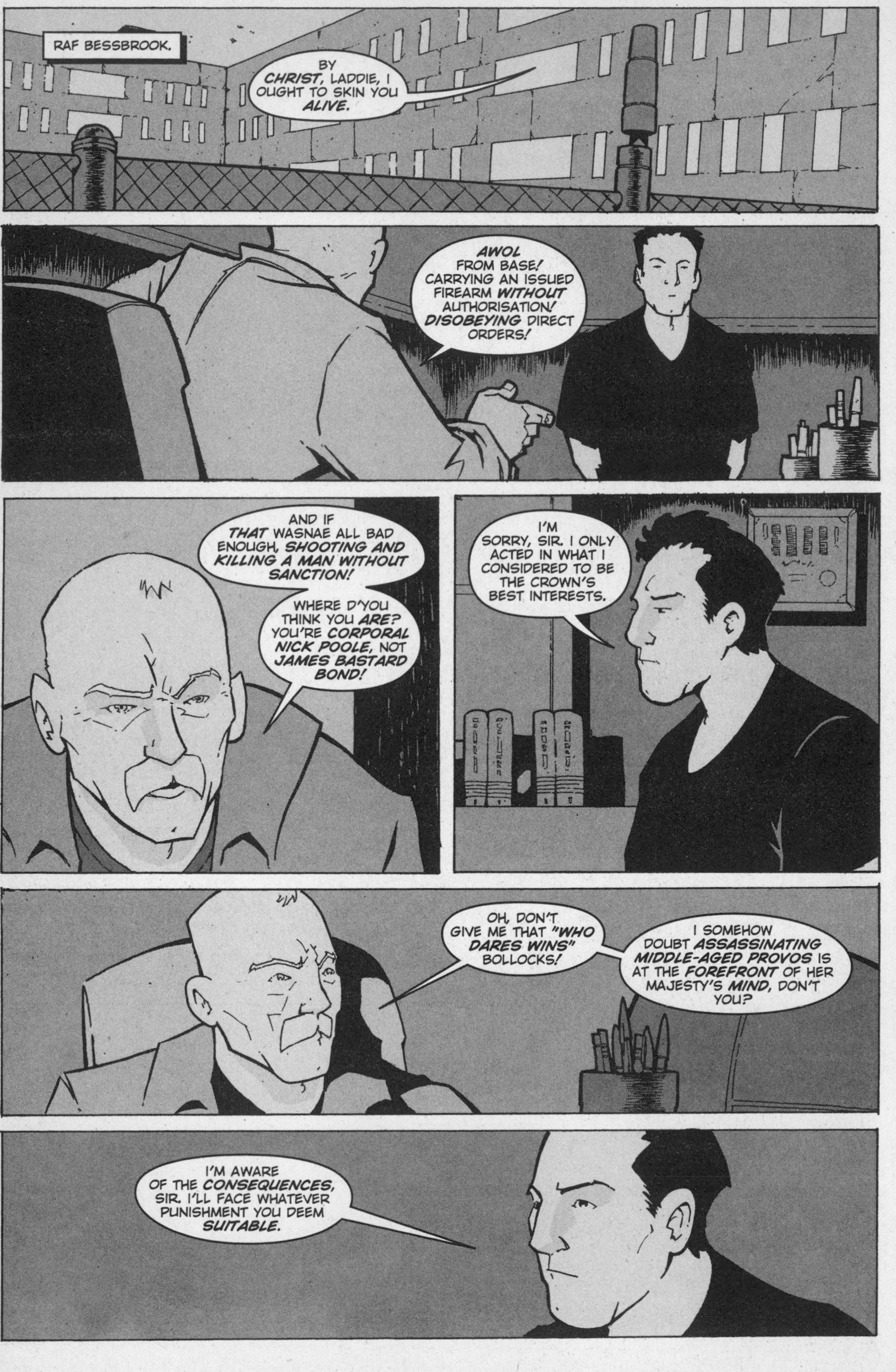
RAF BESSBROOK.
BY CHRIST, LADDIE, I OUGHT TO SKIN YOU ALIVE.
AWOL FROM BASE! CARRYING AN ISSUED FIREARM WITHOUT AUTHORISATION! DISOBEYING DIRECT ORDERS!
AND IF THAT WASNAE ALL BAD ENOUGH, SHOOTING AND KILLING A MAN WITHOUT SANCTION!
WHERE D'YOU THINK YOU ARE? YOU'RE CORPORAL NICK POOLE, NOT JAMES BASTARD BOND!
I'M SORRY, SIR. I ONLY ACTED IN WHAT I CONSIDERED TO BE THE CROWN'S BEST INTERESTS.
OH, DON'T GIVE ME THAT "WHO DARES WINS" BOLLOCKS!
I SOMEHOW DOUBT ASSASSINATING MIDDLE-AGED PROVOS IS AT THE FOREFRONT OF HER MAJESTY'S MIND, DON'T YOU?
I'M AWARE OF THE CONSEQUENCES, SIR. I'LL FACE WHATEVER PUNISHMENT YOU DEEM SUITABLE.

AYE, I THINK YOU *WOULD*.

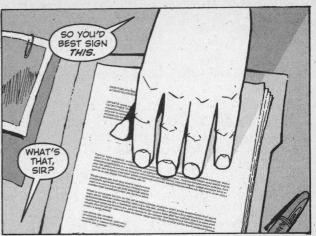
SO YOU'D BEST SIGN *THIS*.

WHAT'S THAT, SIR?

IT'S A *DEBRIEF STATEMENT*, CORPORAL.

IT FOLLOWS YOUR SUCCESSFUL EXECUTION OF *OPERATION DAUGHTER*, THE EMERGENCY *CONTINGENCY MISSION* TO PROTECT THE LIFE OF LAUREN MULLEN DURING THE UNIVERSITY *BOMB HOAX*, WHICH I FORMULATED AND SANCTIONED AT *NINETEEN-TWELVE* THIS EVENING.

TWO MINUTES AFTER WE LEARNT OF THE CALL TO *PSNI*.

JUST *SIGN* THE BLOODY THING, LADDIE, BEFORE I COME TO MY *SENSES*.

YES, SIR.

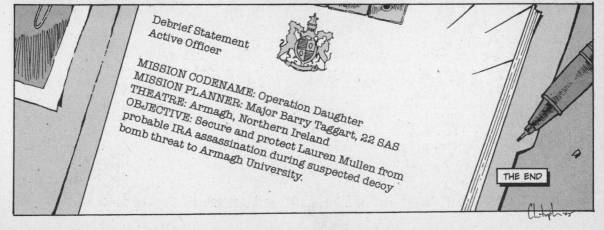
Debrief Statement
Active Officer

MISSION CODENAME: Operation Daughter
MISSION PLANNER: Major Barry Taggart, 22 SAS
THEATRE: Armagh, Northern Ireland
OBJECTIVE: Secure and protect Lauren Mullen from probable IRA assassination during suspected decoy bomb threat to Armagh University.

THE END

Supplementary material
Issue #1

GLOSSARY OF TERMS

As part of its emphasis on realism, Queen & Country uses many abbreviations, acronyms and terms found in the everyday life of a Government agency, such as D-Ops, Conops, PUS, FCO and more. Regular readers have become accustomed to these terms over time, but the unfamiliar setting of Declassified, Volume III requires a whole new set of abbreviations and slang. We hope you find the following glossary helpful.

ULSTER

Northern Ireland, specifically the six counties politically connected to the United Kingdom.
"Ulster" is historically the name of a region consisting of nine counties, of which three are not part of the UK, being instead part of the Republic of Ireland. The use of "Ulster" as a catch-all term for the British-controlled part of Northern Ireland is therefore controversial, regarded by many Republicans as insulting, and is no longer used in official public parlance. Nevertheless, the term is still commonly used by the British Army and many locals, especially Unionists, to refer to Northern Ireland as a whole.

ÉIRE/REPUBLIC OF IRELAND

That part of Ireland not ruled by, or part of, the United Kingdom. Technically, "Éire" is the correct name for these 26 counties, as "Republic of Ireland" is a description rather than a name. However, "Éire" is also the modern Irish name for all Ireland, and its use when discussing only the Republic has therefore come to be regarded by many as condescending. "Republic of Ireland" is now the state's de facto name in all but legal terms.

UNIONIST

One who believes Northern Ireland should remain part of, and politically allied to, the United Kingdom.

DUP

The Democratic Unionist Party. Led by the Rev. Ian Paisley, its membership consists mainly (but not exclusively) of Protestants and is Unionist.

REPUBLICAN/NATIONALIST

One who believes the United Kingdom should renounce all claim to rule over any part of Ireland, and that all Ireland should be united under Republican rule.

SINN FÉIN

The primary counterpart to the DUP, and the political wing of the IRA. Led by Jerry Adams, its membership consists mainly (but not exclusively) of Catholics and is Republican.

SAS

The Special Air Service, an elite special forces regiment of the British Army. Officially titled "22 Special Air Service (SAS)" to differentiate it from the two volunteer SAS regiments (21 and 23), but almost exclusively referred to simply as "The SAS". The SAS consists of four Sabre Squadrons, each of which is divided into four separate 16-man "Troops" with different specialist areas (Air, Boat, Mobility and Mountain). Each Squadron also spends 6-9 months acting as the regiment's primary Counter-Revolutionary Warfare unit on a rotation basis. An SAS soldier is known as a "Trooper".

ULSTER TROOP

A "ghost troop" consisting of around twenty SAS troopers, rotated every six months from their usual regiment postings. The average Trooper serves six months in Ulster Troop for every four years of service.

THE GROUP

Intelligence and Security Group (Northern Ireland). The joint name for Ulster Troop and 14 Int, over which presides a single Commanding Officer. In theory, the RUC (and now PSNI) are also part of The Group, and to be regarded as trusted allies. In practice, this is rarely the case.

14 INT

14th Intelligence Unit, a covert intelligence-gathering arm of the British Army formed for and operating exclusively in Northern Ireland. 14th Int operatives are trained by the SAS.

RTU'D

Returned To Unit. Each SAS Trooper is recruited from an existing regiment of the British armed forces, and officially are still part of that regiment. Troopers may be RTU'd for various reasons, the most common being dismissal or retirement from the SAS. After a debriefing period, they are returned to active duty in their "old" regiment.

BANDIT COUNTRY

The region of South Armagh, as originally nicknamed by Merlyn Rees (Secretary of State for Northern Ireland 1974-76) and informally adopted by the British Army. South Armagh is almost exclusively Catholic and Republican. Until the Good Friday peace agreement, South Armagh was the most dangerous operational theatre in the world for any member of the British armed forces, including the SAS.

PROVOS

The Provisional IRA, the longest-running and best-known branch of the IRA. No longer officially active after the Good Friday peace agreement, their baton of violent resistance has been taken up instead by the Real IRA and other, smaller IRA groups. These distinctions are often ignored by members of the British armed forces, who refer to any Republican militant as a Provo.

PADDY

Derogatory term for any Irish person, particularly IRA members, commonly used by SAS Troopers.

RUC

The Royal Ulster Constabulary, the police force of Northern Ireland. Regarded by Republicans as little better than British soldiers, in 2001 the RUC was disbanded in an attempt to remove the long-standing negative associations the name carried in many people's memories. It was replaced by the PSNI.

PSNI

The Police Service of Northern Ireland, formed in 2001 to replace the RUC. In practice, little about the PSNI is different to the RUC.

BESSBROOK INTERNATIONAL/THE MILL

Bessbrook Mill HQ is the base of operations for Ulster Troop and other British armed forces operating in the southern counties of Northern Ireland. The "International" nickname refers to the large amount of air traffic around Bessbrook - during the 1980s, after surface travel in the southern counties was all but abandoned by British armed forces, Bessbrook was the busiest heliport in Europe.

ARMAGH

The capital of County Armagh. While not part of South Armagh, Armagh itself was still regarded as a hotbed of IRA activity before the Good Friday peace agreement. Much of the city's tension comes from Armagh's unique religious position. Regarded as the spiritual home of all Ireland, it has a large mixed Protestant and Catholic population, and is the seat of Archbishops from both the Church of Ireland and Roman Catholic Church.

ANTONY JOHNSTON - MAY 10 2005, ENGLAND

ANTONY JOHNSTON

Antony Johnston was born and raised in England. He is the critically-acclaimed author of THREE DAYS IN EUROPE, CLOSER, SPOOKED, JULIUS, THE LONG HAUL, and F-STOP. Antony is also the author of the illustrated prose novel FRIGHTENING CURVES (winner of Best Horror Novel at the American Independent Publishing Awards) and the graphic novels ROSEMARY'S BACKPACK (with artist Drew Gilbert)

He has also adapted many prose works by Alan Moore into comics form. He also has a new ongoing comic series, WASTELAND, with QUEEN & COUNTRY collaborator, Christopher Mitten. Antony lives in the south of England with his girlfriend, an iMac and a wardrobe that steadfastly refuses to acknowledge colour.

www.mostlyblack.com

CHRISTOPHER MITTEN

Christopher Mitten is the accomplished illustrator of the graphic novels LAST EXIT BEFORE TOLL and THE TOMB. He resides just outside of Chicago, Illinois where he currently splits his time between work on his new ongoing comic series, WASTELAND, with writer Antony Johnston and denying his intense desire to shoot caffeine directly into his eyeballs.

www.christophermitten.com

GREG RUCKA

Born in San Francisco, Greg Rucka was raised on the Monterey Peninsula. He is the author of several novels, including one featuring characters from this very series, as well as several comic books, for which he has won three Eisner Awards. He resides in Portland, Oregon, with his wife, Jennifer, and their children, Elliot and Dashiell.

www.gregrucka.com

ACKNOWLEDGEMENTS:

Antony and Christopher would like to thank the following people, for invaluable help with research and reference: Eoin Cleland, Alan Cleland, Patrick McGuigan and Louise McCarton.

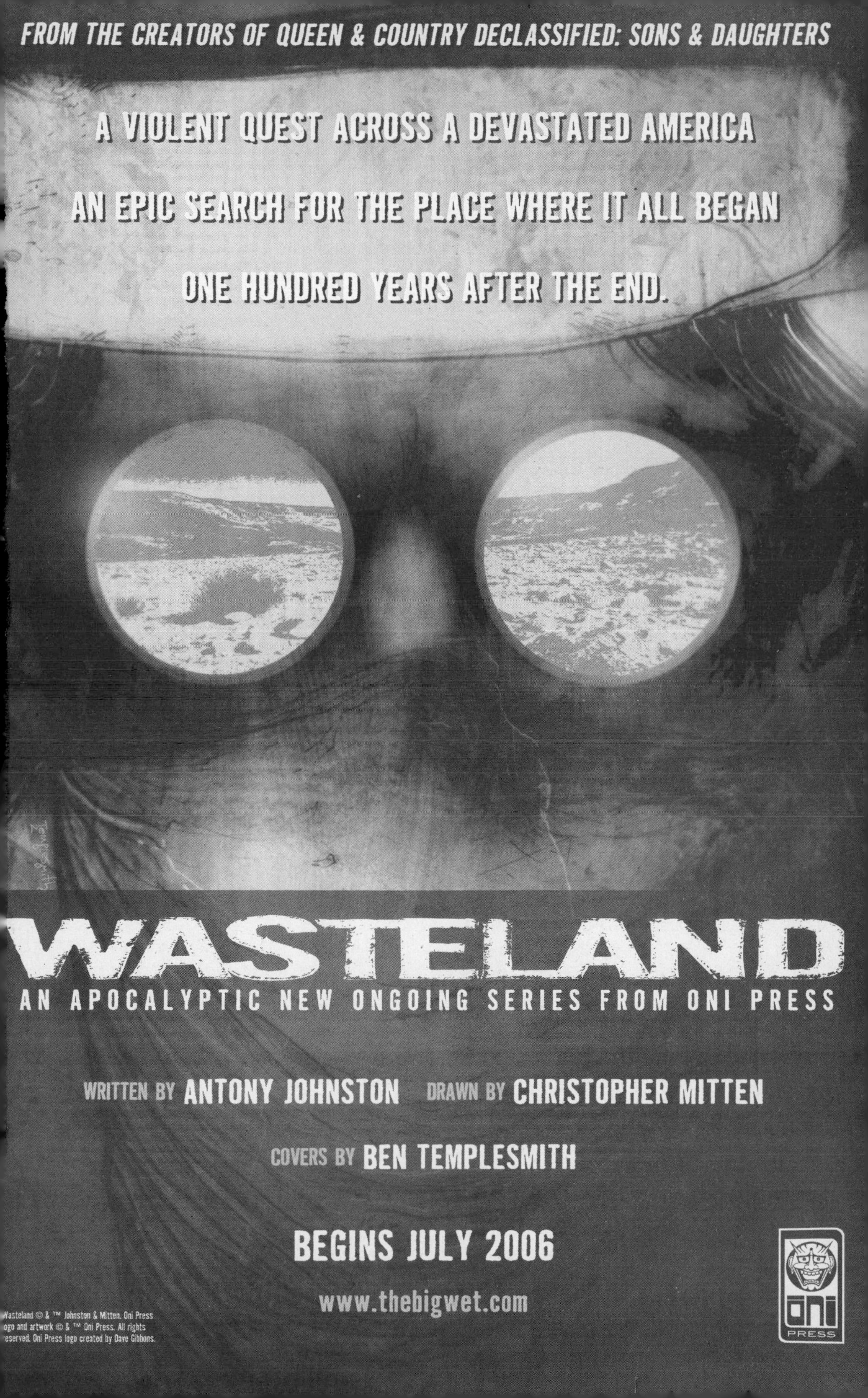
FROM THE CREATORS OF QUEEN & COUNTRY DECLASSIFIED: SONS & DAUGHTERS
A VIOLENT QUEST ACROSS A DEVASTATED AMERICA
AN EPIC SEARCH FOR THE PLACE WHERE IT ALL BEGAN
ONE HUNDRED YEARS AFTER THE END.
WASTELAND
AN APOCALYPTIC NEW ONGOING SERIES FROM ONI PRESS
WRITTEN BY ANTONY JOHNSTON DRAWN BY CHRISTOPHER MITTEN
COVERS BY BEN TEMPLESMITH
BEGINS JULY 2006
www.thebigwet.com
oni PRESS
Wasteland © & ™ Johnston & Mitten. Oni Press logo and artwork © & ™ Oni Press. All rights reserved. Oni Press logo created by Dave Gibbons.

QUEEN & COUNTRY

QUEEN & COUNTRY

QUEEN & COUNTRY
OPERATION: CRYSTAL BALL
GREG RUCKA
LEANDRO FERNANDEZ

QUEEN & COUNTRY

QUEEN & COUNTRY
OPERATION: STORM FRONT

QUEEN & COUNTRY
GREG RUCKA
MIKE HAWTHORNE

QUEEN & COUNTRY
OPERATION: SADDLEBAGS

QUEEN & COUNTRY
DECLASSIFIED

QUEEN & COUNTRY

www.onipress.com

"You'll be hard-pressed to find an espionage thriller as gritty, as prescient, as *real* as *Queen & Country*... Grade: A."
– Entertainment Weekly

GREG RUCKA'S

★ Eisner Award-winning graphic novel series ★

QUEEN & COUNTRY

Vol. 1
Operation: Broken Ground
art by Steve Rolston,
and Stan Sakai
128 pages, black-and-white interiors
$11.95 US
ISBN 1-929998-21-X

Vol. 2
Operation: Morningstar
art by Brian Hurtt, Bryan O'Malley, and
Christine Norrie
88 pages, black-and-white interiors
$8.95 US
ISBN 1-929998-35-X

Vol. 3
Operation: Crystal Ball
art by Leandro Fernandez
154 pages, black-and-white interiors
$14.95 US
ISBN 1-929998-49-X

Vol. 4
Operation: Blackwall
art by J. Alexander
88 pages, black-and-white interiors
$8.95 US
ISBN 1-929998-68-6

Vol. 5
Operation: Storm Front
art by Carla Speed McNeil
144 pages, black-and-white interiors
$14.95 US
ISBN 1-929998-84-8

Vol. 6
Operation: Dandelion
art by Mike Hawthorne
120 pages, $11.95 US,
mature readers
ISBN 1-929998-97-X

Vol. 7
Operation: Saddlebags
art by Mike Norton & Steve Rolston
144 pages, $14.95 US,
mature readers
ISBN 1-932664-14-9

Declassified
Vol. 1
art by Brian Hurtt
96 pages, black-and-white interiors
$8.95 US
ISBN 1-929998-58-9

Declassified
Vol. 2
art by Brian Hurtt
96 pages, black-and-white interiors
$8.95 US
ISBN 1-929998-58-9

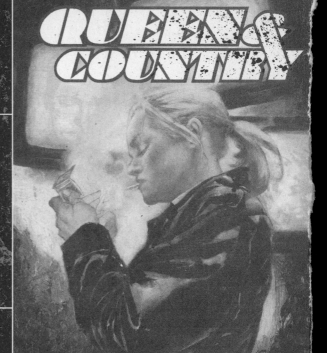